GIFTED AND TALENTED TEST PREPARATION

COGAT® GRADE 2

300+ Questions /
2 Full-Length Practice Tests
Level 8

Savant Test Prep™
www.SavantPrep.com

Please leave a review for this book!

Thank you for purchasing this resource.
If you would take a moment to kindly leave a
review on the website where you purchased this publication,
we would appreciate it.

Check out our collection of COGAT® prep books:

TABLE OF CONTENTS

INTRODUCTION

COGAT® GENERAL INFORMATION

- COGAT® stands for Cognitive Abilities Test®. It measures students' reasoning skills and problem-solving skills.
- It provides educators with an overall assessment of students' academic strengths and weaknesses.
    - The test is sometimes used together with the ITBS™ (a.k.a. Iowa Test) for this purpose.
- It is commonly used as a screener for gifted and talented programs.
    - Gifted and Talented (G&T) selection sometimes requires a teacher recommendation as well.
- The test is usually administered in a group setting.
- A teacher (or other school associate) administers the test, reading the directions. (Computerized versions of the test are also available.)
- Please check with your school / testing site regarding its testing procedures, as these may differ.

COGAT® LEVEL 8 FORMAT

- Students in second grade take the COGAT® Level 8. (Level 7 is for first grade. Level 9 is for third grade.)
- The test has 154 questions.
- The test is divided into 3 main parts, each called a "Battery". Each Battery has three question types. See chart below.

VERBAL BATTERY	NON-VERBAL BATTERY	QUANTITATIVE BATTERY
Picture Analogies: 18 Questions	Figure Analogies: 18 Questions	Number Puzzles: 14 Questions
Picture Classification: 18 Questions	Figure Classification: 18 Questions	Number Series: 18 Questions
Sentence Completion: 18 Questions	Paper Folding: 14 Questions	Number Analogies: 18 Questions

- Often, schools administer one Battery per day, allowing approximately 45 minutes per Battery.
- Students have around 15 minutes to complete each question type (for example, students would have around 15 minutes to complete Picture Analogies).
- See pages 6-11 for examples and explanations of each question type.

COGAT® SCORING

- Students receive points for correct answers. Points are not deducted for incorrect answers. (Therefore, students should at least guess versus leaving a question blank.)
- In general, schools have a "cut-off" COGAT® score, which they consider together with additional criteria, for gifted & talented acceptance. This varies by school.
- This score is usually at least 98%. (However, some schools accept scores 95% or even 85%.)
- A score of 98% means that your child scored as well as, or better than, 98% of children in his/her testing group.
- COGAT® scores are available for the entire test and can be broken down by Battery.
- Depending on the school/program, such a "cut-off" score may only be required on one or two of the Batteries (and not on the test overall).
- It is essential to check with your school/program for their acceptance procedures.

(The COGAT® Practice Tests in this book can not yield these percentiles because they have not been given to a large enough group of students to produce an accurate comparison / calculation.)

HOW TO USE THIS BOOK

1. Go over examples and explanations (p.6 - 11).

2. Do Practice Test 1.
- • Do these questions together with your child, especially if this is your child's first exposure to COGAT®-prep questions.
  - Talk about what the question is asking your child to do.
- • Questions progress in difficulty.
  - The first few questions are quite simple.
- • Do at least one section (Verbal / Non-Verbal/ Quantitative) per day.
- • Do not assign a time limit.
- • Go over the answers using the Answer Key (p. 107).
  - For questions missed, go over the answers again, discussing what makes the correct answer better than the other choices.

3. Do Practice Test 2.
- • If your child progressed easily through Practice Test 1, then see how well your child can do on Practice Test 2 without your help.
- • If your child needed assistance with much of Practice Test 1, then continue to assist your child with Practice Test 2.
- • Do at least one section (Verbal / Non-Verbal/ Quantitative) per day.
- • If you wish to assign a time limit, assign around 15 minutes per question type.
- • Go over the answers using the Answer Key (p. 107-109).
  - For questions missed, go over the answers again, discussing what makes the correct answer better than the other choices.

4. Go to our website, www.SavantPrep.com, for FREE 10 bonus practice questions (PDF format).

GET FREE 10 BONUS PRACTICE QUESTIONS (PDF) !
GO TO WWW.SAVANTPREP.COM AND GET THEM TODAY.

TEST-TAKING TIPS

- • Ensure your child listens carefully to the directions, especially in the Sentence Completion section.
- • Make sure (s)he does not rush through questions. (There is no prize for finishing first!) Tell your child to look carefully at the question. Then, tell your child to look at each answer choice before marking his/her answer.
  - If you notice your child continuing to rush through the questions, tell him/ her to point to each part of the question. Then, point to each answer choice.
- • If (s)he does not know the answer, then use the process of elimination. Cross out any answer choices which are clearly incorrect, then choose from those remaining.
- • This tip/suggestion is entirely at your discretion. You may wish to offer some sort of special motivation to encourage your child to do his/her best. An extra incentive of, for example, an art set, a building block set, or a special outing can go a long way in motivating young learners!
- • The night before testing, it is imperative that children have enough sleep, without any interruptions. (Think about the difference in your brain function with a good night's sleep vs. without. The same goes for your child's brain function.)
- • The morning before the test, ensure your child eats a healthy breakfast with protein and complex carbs. Do not let them eat sugar, chocolate, etc.
- • If you can choose the time your child will take the test (for example, if (s)he will take the test individually, instead of at school with a group), opt for a morning testing session, when your child will be most alert.

QUESTION EXAMPLES

- Here is an overview of the nine COGAT® question types.
- This section has <u>simple</u> examples, to introduce your child to test concepts.
  - Do these examples together with your child. Read him/her the directions.
- Below the questions are explanations for parents.

1. PICTURE ANALOGIES (VERBAL BATTERY) / p. 12 and p. 61 in the Practice Tests

• **Directions (read to child):** The pictures in the top boxes go together in some way. Look at the bottom boxes. One box is empty. Look at the row of pictures next to the boxes. These are the answer choices. Which one of these choices goes with the picture in the bottom box like the pictures in the top boxes go together?

○   ○   ○   ○

• **Explanation (for parents):** Your child must figure out how the images in top set of boxes are related and belong together. Then, (s)he must figure out which answer choice would go with the bottom left image so that the bottom set would have the same analogous relationship as the top set. (The small arrows demonstrate that the images go together.)

• One strategy is to try to define a "rule" to describe how the top set belongs together. Then, take this "rule" and use it with the bottom picture. Look at the answer choices, and figure out which answer would make the bottom set follow your "rule."

• **Using the above question as an example, say to your child:**
In this question, we see a spider and a web. A spider's home is its web. A rule would be, "the thing in the first box has as its home the thing in the second box." On the bottom we see a bird. Let's try the answer choices with our rule. A flower is not correct because a bird's home is not a flower, nor is a bench or another bird. A nest is correct because it's a bird's home.

• Another similar strategy is to try to come up with a sentence to describe how the top set belongs together. Then, use this sentence with the bottom picture. Look at the answer choices, and figure out which answer would make the sentence work with this bottom set. With both strategies, if more than one answer choice works, then you need a more specific rule/sentence.

• The table below outlines the logic used in verbal analogies (on the COGAT®, as well as in verbal analogies, in general). While the COGAT® Level 8 uses pictures (not words) in verbal analogies, we suggest reading the questions and answer choices to your child. This will help familiarize him/her with analogy logic.

Question (say below & each 'Choice' to child)	Choice 1	Choice 2	Choice 3	Choice 4	*Analogy Logic*
1. Spider -is to- Web as Bird -is to- ?	Flower	Bench	Nest ✓	Bird	*Animal:* *Animal's Home*
2. Acorns -are to- Squirrel as Seeds -are to- ?	Grass	Bird ✓	Fish	Snake	*Animal:* *Animal's Food*
3. Calf -is to- Cow as Cub -is to- ?	Tiger ✓	Horse	Goose	Bull	*Animal Baby:* *Animal Adult*
4. Lion -is to- Fur as Snake -is to- ?	Lizard	Hair	Fangs	Scales ✓	*Animal:* *Animal's Covering*
5. Happy -is to- Sad as Wet -is to- ?	Damp	Clean	Water	Dry ✓	*"X": "X" 's Opposite*
6. Tiger -is to- Cheetah as Butterfly -is to- ?	Bird	Bat	Moth ✓	Jaguar	*Similar: Similar*

Question (say below & each 'Choice' to child)	Choice 1	Choice 2	Choice 3	Choice 4	Analogy Logic
7. Flower -is to- Bouquet as Kernel -is to- ?	Snack	Plant	Corn Cob ✓	Crop	Part: Whole
8. Ship -is to- Port as Car -is to- ?	Truck	Garage ✓	Marina	Wheel	Object: Location
9. Pencil -is to- Paper as Paint -is to- ?	Wall ✓	Color	Red	Light	Object: Object Used With
10. Lumber -is to- Fence as Paper -is to- ?	Log	Branch	Tree	Book ✓	Object: Product That Object Is Put Together To Make
11. Doctor -is to- Stethoscope as Carpenter -is to- ?	Boot	Builder	Cabinet	Hammer ✓	Worker Who Uses Object: Object
12. Cheese -is to- Refrigerator as Ice -is to- ?	Snow	Toaster	Freezer ✓	Cube	Object: Item Used to Store/Hold Object
13. Box -is to- Cube as Globe -is to- ?	Prism	Sphere ✓	Oval	Pentagon	Object: Similar Shape
14. Straw -is to- Juice as Spoon -is to- ?	Cereal ✓	Salad	Steak	Sandwich	Utensil: Object Utensil Is Used With
15. Egg -is to- Chicken as Milk -is to- ?	Chick	Cheese	Rooster	Cow ✓	Food/Drink: Source of Food/Drink
16. Ambulance -is to- Paramedic as Tractor -is to- ?	Doctor	Teacher	Scientist	Farmer ✓	Vehicle: User

2. PICTURE CLASSIFICATION (VERBAL BATTERY) / p. 25 and p. 67 in the Practice Tests

• **Directions (read to child):** The top row shows three pictures that are alike in some way. Look at the bottom row. There are four pictures. Which picture in the bottom row goes best with the pictures in the top row?

• **Explanation (for parents):** Together with your child, try to figure out a "rule" describing how the top pictures are alike and belong together. Then, apply the "rule" to each answer choice to determine which one follows it. If your child finds that more than one choice follows the rule, then a more specific rule is needed.

• **Using the above question as an example, say to your child:** In the top row, we see a ladybug, a party hat, and a dog. What do these have in common? It may be hard to see at first. Let's have another look. Each of these have spots. This is how they are alike. The only answer choice that has spots is the cheetah.

You can help your child improve classification using items you see in everyday life or in books. The table on the next page lists common themes for Picture Classification (which also appear in Picture Analogies and Sentence Completion questions). Under the logic is an example question. Read the first list of 3 words to your child. Then, next to it, read the 4 choices to your child. Which one of the choices goes best with the first list?

• The table below outlines some of the logic themes used in COGAT® Picture Classification questions. While the COGAT® Level 8 uses pictures (not words) in classification questions, we suggest reading the questions and answer choices to your child. Through simple examples, this will help familiarize him/her with basic classification logic. The classification logic/explanation is in the third column.

-Step 1: Read the three words on the left to your child. Tell him/her that these words belong together in some way.

-Step 2: Read the four words on the right to your child. Ask him/her which one of these goes best with the first three words. The answer has a check (✓). Following is a brief explanation of the question's logic in *italics*.

Question (read to child)	Answer Choices (read to child)	Classification Logic / Explanation
1. Cave / Hive / Web	Spider / Nest ✓ / Vet / Bat	*Animal Homes*
2. Butterfly / Ant / Bee	Worm / Horse / Bird / Dragonfly ✓	*Animal Types (Insects)*
3. Forest / Jungle / Desert	Tree / Valley / Rainforest ✓ / City	*Habitats*
4. Lemon / Grape / Apple	Strawberry ✓ / Farm / Sweet / Lettuce	*Kinds of Food (Fruit)*
5. Scientist / Nurse / Detective	Superhero / Teenager / Pilot ✓ / Fairy	*Jobs*
6. Sock / Skate / Boot	Slipper ✓ / Cap / Mitten / Toe	*Clothes/Shoes (Worn On Feet)*
7. Jet / Hot Air Balloon / Helicopter	Ship / Airport / Bird / Airplane ✓	*Transportation (Air Travel)*
8. Ruler / Scale / Measuring Tape	Thermometer ✓ / Number / TV / Pen	*Object Use (Used to Measure)*
9. Pillow / Blanket / Mattress	Towel / Chair / Sheet ✓ / Table	*Object Location (Found on Beds)*
10. Fire / Sun / Stove	Cookie / Toaster ✓ / Beach / Camp	*Object Characteristics (Give Heat)*
11. Planet / Ball / Globe	Country / Goal / Bubble ✓ / Racetrack	*Object Shape (Spherical)*

3. SENTENCE COMPLETION (VERBAL BATTERY) / p. 38 and p. 73 in the Practice Tests

• **Directions (read to child):** Listen to the question, then choose the best answer.

Which one of these shows a pair?

     ○   ○   ○   ○

• **Explanation (for parents):** Unlike Picture Analogies and Picture Classification, Sentence Completion questions have different directions. The above example is a very simple one. (The answer is C.) The questions in this book's two practice tests will be more challenging.

• It is imperative that your child listens carefully to these questions. COGAT® administrators will not repeat the questions.
• If listening is challenging for your child - tell him/her to repeat the directions back to you.
• Remind your child to listen to the entire question. (Some children will stop listening if they think they already know the answer.)
• Tell him/her to pay special attention to "negative" words like "not" or "no". (The two practice tests include questions like this.)

4. FIGURE ANALOGIES (NON-VERBAL BATTERY) / p. 18 and p. 78 in the Practice Tests

• **Directions (read to child):** The pictures in the top boxes go together in some way. Look at the bottom boxes. One box is empty. Look at the row of pictures next to the boxes. These are the answer choices. Which one of these choices goes with the picture in the bottom box like the pictures in the top box go together?

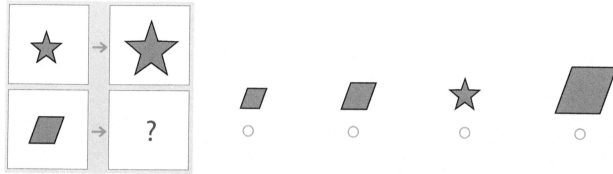

• **Explanation:** In the directions, the word "picture" means a "figure" consisting of one or more shapes/lines/etc. As with Picture Analogies, try to define a "rule" to describe how the top set belongs together. With Figure Analogies, however, make your "rule" describe a "change" that occurs from the top left box to the top right box. Next, take this "rule" describing the change, and apply it to the bottom picture. Then, look at the answer choices to determine which one would make the bottom set also follow your "rule."

• **Using the above question as an example, say to your child:** In the top left box we see 1 star. In the top right box, we also see a star, but it has gotten bigger. Let's come up with a rule to describe how the picture has changed from left to right. From left to right, the shape gets bigger. On the bottom is a parallelogram. Let's look at the answer choices and see if any fit our rule. The first choice does not - the shape is smaller. The second choice does not - the shape is the same size. The third choice does not - it is a different shape. The last choice does - it is the same shape as the bottom box, but it is bigger.

• Below are examples of basic "changes" seen in Figure Analogies. Basic questions, like the above example and #1-#9 below, have one "change". While more advanced questions, like #10, and in the book's practice tests, have two changes (or changes that are not as obvious). See if your child can explain the changes below. At the end is a brief explanation.

1.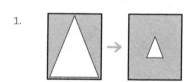

2.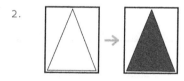

3.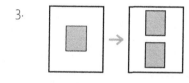

4.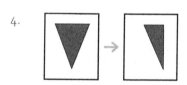

5.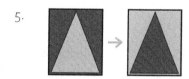

6.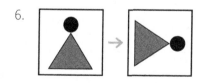

7.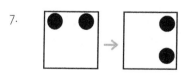

8.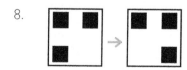

9.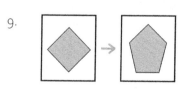

10.

1. Size (gets smaller)
2. Color (white to gray)
3. Quantity (plus 1)
4. Whole to Half
5. Color Reversal
6. Rotation (clockwise, 90°)

7. Rotation (clockwise, 90°)
8. Rotation -or- Mirror Image / "Flip"
9. Number of Shape Sides (shape with +1 side)
10. Two Changes: Rotation (clockwise, 90°)
    and Color Reversal

5. FIGURE CLASSIFICATION (NON-VERBAL BATTERY) / p. 32 and p. 84 in the Practice Tests

• **Directions (read to child):** The top row shows three pictures that are alike in some way. Look at the bottom row. There are four pictures. Which picture in the bottom row goes best with the pictures in the top row?

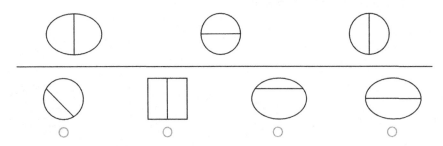

• **Explanation (for parents):** Together with your child, try to figure out a "rule" describing how the top pictures are alike and belong together. Then, apply the "rule" to each answer choice to determine which one follows it. If your child finds that more than one choice follows the rule, then a more specific rule is needed.

• **Using the above question as an example, say to your child:** Here we see 1 oval divided in half, 1 circle divided in half, and 1 circle divided in half. What is a rule that describes how they are alike? They are all round and divided in half. In the bottom row, which choice follows this rule? Choice 1 and 3 are round and divided, but not divided in half. Choice 2 is divided in half, but it is not round. Choice 4 is round and divided in half.

This list outlines some basic logic used in Figure Classification questions. (Practice test questions will be more challenging.)

How shapes are divided (Here, shapes are divided in quarters, with 1 part filled in.)	
How many sides the shapes have (Here, it is 4.)	
Do shapes have all rounded corners or straight corners? Or, no corners at all?	
Direction shapes are facing (Here, they face right.)	
Color / Design inside shape (Here, there are dots.)	
Shape quantity in each shape group (Here, 2 shapes in each group.)	
Shape group, with a set order to the group (Here, it's circle-diamond-square.)	

6. PAPER FOLDING (NON-VERBAL BATTERY)

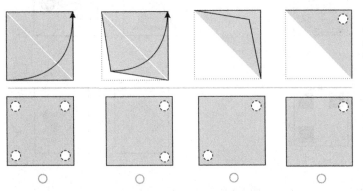

• **Directions (read to child):** The top row of pictures shows a sheet of paper. The paper was folded, then something was cut out. Which picture in the bottom row shows how the paper would look after its unfolded?

• **Explanation (read to child):** The first choice has too many holes. In the second choice, the holes are not in the correct position. The third choice has the correct number of holes and in the correct position. The last choice only shows the hole on top.

• **Tip:** It is common for children to initially struggle with Paper Folding - it is not an activity most children have much experience with. First, have a look at the Paper Folding questions in this book. Then, demonstrate using hands-on examples. Get sheets of real paper, and let your child experiment with:

- different fold directions (horizontal, vertical, diagonal)

- different fold quantity (folding once vs. twice)
- different placement of holes

7. NUMBER SERIES (QUANTITATIVE BATTERY) / p. 51 and p. 102 in the Practice Tests

- **Directions (read to child):** Which rod should go in the place of the missing rod to finish the pattern?

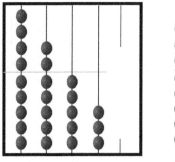 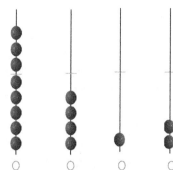

- **Explanation (read to child):** Before the missing rod, the other rods have made a pattern that we need to figure out. Then, we will complete the pattern with the correct answer choice. From left to right, we see that with each rod the number of beads goes down by 2. The rods go: 9–7–5-3- ? This means that the missing rod needs 1 bead (Choice C).

Below is a list of common Number Series patterns.

Basic Patterns	Number of Beads
• +1	1, 2, 3, 4, 5
• -1	5, 4, 3, 2, 1
• A/B/A/B	1, 2, 1, 2
• A/B/C/D/C/B/A	1, 2, 3, 4, 3, 2, 1

Challenging Patterns	Number of Beads
• A / X / A+1 / X / A+2	4, 1, 5, 1, 6, 1, 7 (note how 1 repeats every other time; the other numbers increase by +1)
• A / X / A-1 / X / A-2	8, 3, 7, 3, 6, 3, 5 (note how 3 repeats every other time; the other numbers decrease by -1)
• +1 / +2 / +1 / +2	1, 2, 4, 5, 7, 8, 10 (note how the pattern alternates: +1, +2, +1, +2)

8. NUMBER PUZZLES (QUANTITATIVE BATTERY) / p. 49 and p. 95 in the Practice Tests

- **Directions (read to child):** Which number would be in place of the question mark so that both of the sides of this equal sign are the same?

- **Explanation:** This section is straightforward. Make sure your child pays attention to the plus and minus signs.

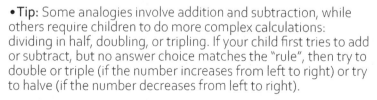

9. NUMBER ANALOGIES (QUANTITATIVE BATTERY) / p. 56 and p. 98 in the Practice Tests

- **Directions (read to child):** The pictures in the top boxes go together in some way. Look at the bottom boxes. One box is empty. Look at the row of answer choices next to the boxes. Which one of these choices goes with the picture in the bottom box like the pictures in the top box go together?

- **Explanation (read to child):** In the left box there are 7 objects (stars). In the right box there are 2 objects. From left to right, we see that 5 objects have been taken away. So, the rule here is "5 are taken away" or "-5." In the bottom left box there are 9 objects. If our rule is "5 are taken away," if you have 9 and you take away 5, you get 4. The third answer choice is correct.

- **Tip:** Some analogies involve addition and subtraction, while others require children to do more complex calculations: dividing in half, doubling, or tripling. If your child first tries to add or subtract, but no answer choice matches the "rule", then try to double or triple (if the number increases from left to right) or try to halve (if the number decreases from left to right).

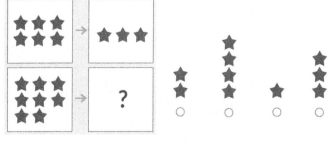

Show your child this example. In the top left box are 6 stars. In top right box are 3 stars. Let's try the rule "take away 3." In the bottom left box are 8 stars. If our rule is "take away 3," then the answer should be 5 stars. However, there isn't an answer choice with 5 stars. Let's look again at the top boxes. If you divide 6 in half, you get 3. Let's try the rule "divide in half." If you take the 8 stars in the bottom left box and divide them in half, you get 4. Choice B has four stars.

- PRACTICE TEST 1 BEGINS ON THE NEXT PAGE-

PICTURE ANALOGIES

Directions (read to child): The pictures in the top boxes go together in some way. Look at the bottom boxes. One box is empty. Look at the row of pictures next to the boxes. These are the answer choices. Which one of these choices goes with the picture in the bottom box like the pictures in the top boxes go together?

Explanation (for parents): A more detailed explanation and another example question is on p.6. If you have not already, look over p.6 (later). Following is an excerpt.

Your child must figure out how the images in the top set of boxes are related and belong together. Then, (s)he must figure out which answer choice would go with the bottom left image so that the bottom set would have the same analogous relationship as the top set. (The small arrows demonstrate that the images go together.)

Example (read this to child): Look at the boxes on top. In the first box, we see a knife. In the second box we see a spoon. (Together, try to come up with a "rule" describing how they are alike and go together.) A knife is a utensil used for eating. A spoon is a utensil used for eating. These two are similar because they are both utensils. Let's look in the bottom box. We see a wrench - it is a type of tool. Now, let's look at the answer choices. Which one goes with the picture of the wrench in the same way that the pictures in the top row go together?

The shovel. The shovel is a type of tool, also. A wrench and a shovel are similar because they are both tools.

1.

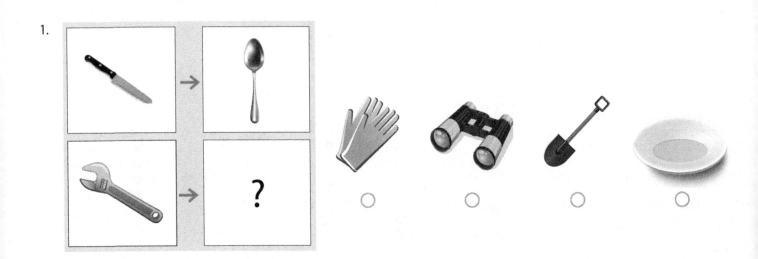

2.

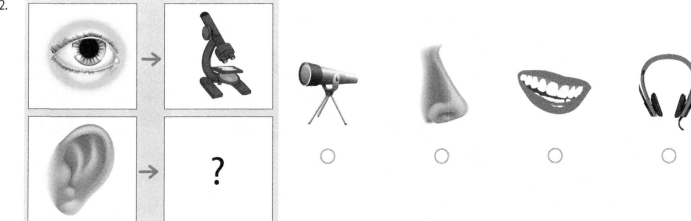

3.

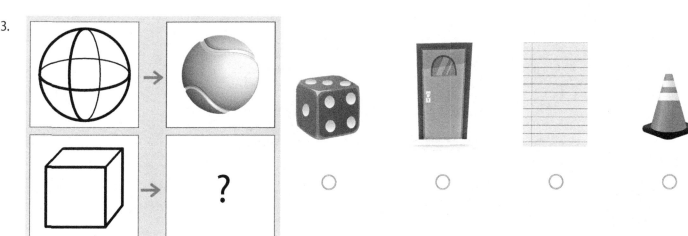

4.

13

5.

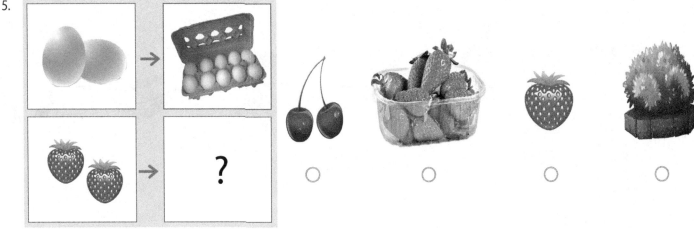

6.

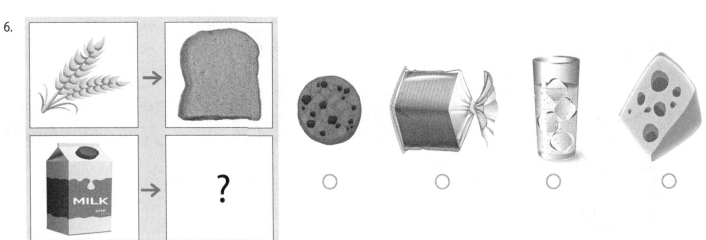

7.

8.

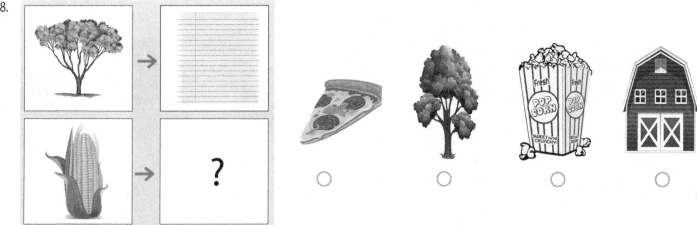

9.

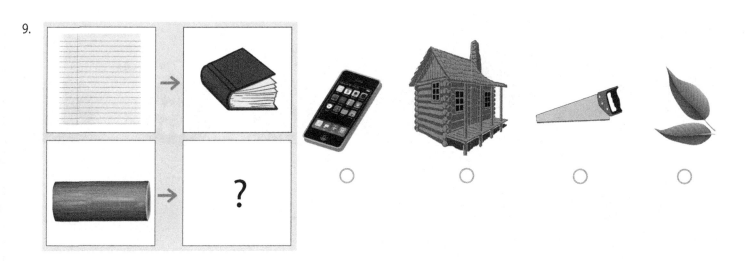

10.

11.

12.

13.

14.

15.

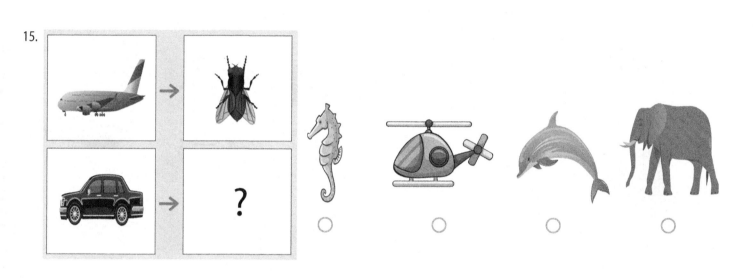

16.

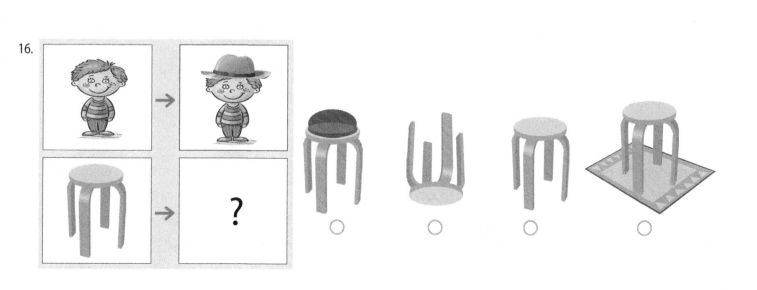

17.

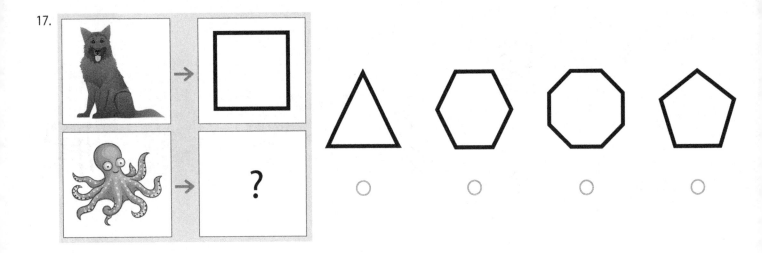

18.

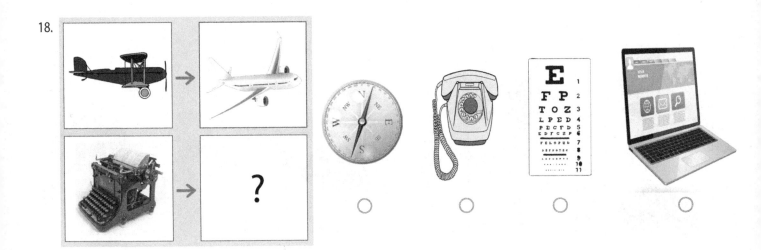

FIGURE ANALOGIES

Directions (read to child): The pictures in the top boxes go together in some way. Look at the bottom boxes. One box is empty. Look at the row of pictures next to the boxes. These are the answer choices. Which one of these choices goes with the picture in the bottom box like the pictures in the top boxes go together?

Explanation (for parents): A more detailed explanation and a Figure Analogies example question is on p. 9. If you have not already, look over p.9 (later). Following is an excerpt. As with Picture Analogies, try to define a "rule" to describe how the top set belongs together. With Figure Analogies, however, make your "rule" describe a "change" that occurs from the top left box to the top right box. Next, take this "rule" describing the change, and apply it to the bottom picture. Then, look at the answer choices to determine which one would make the bottom set also follow your "rule."

1.

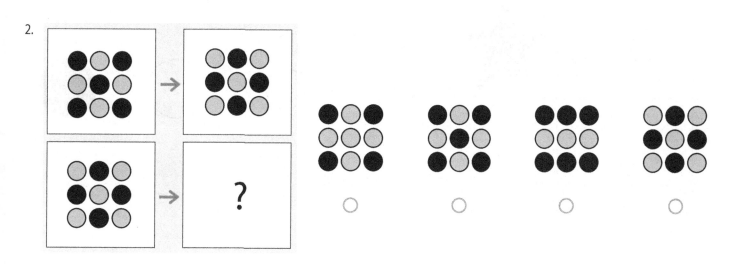

2.

3.

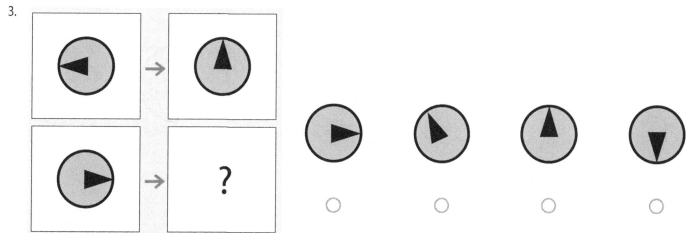

19

4.

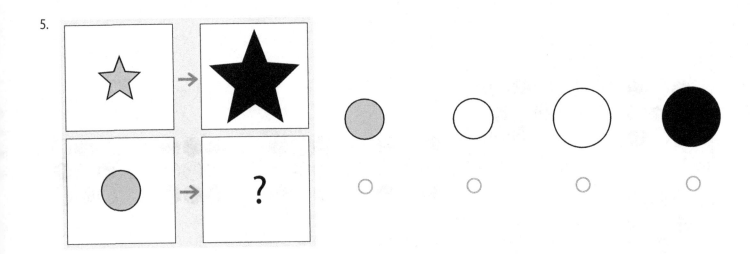

5.

6.

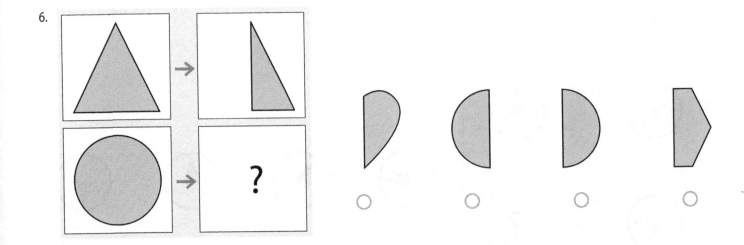

7.

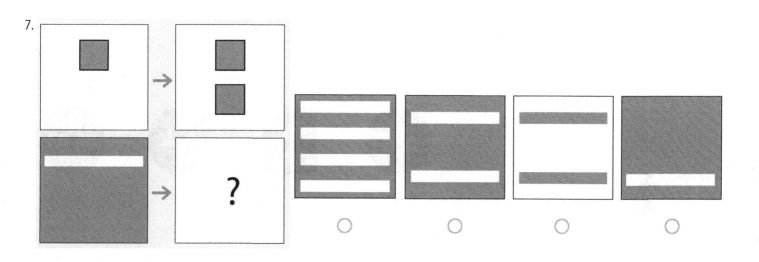

8.

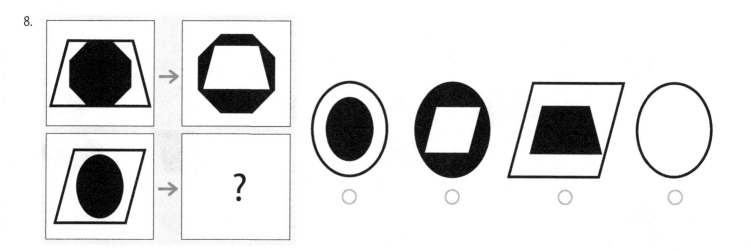

9.

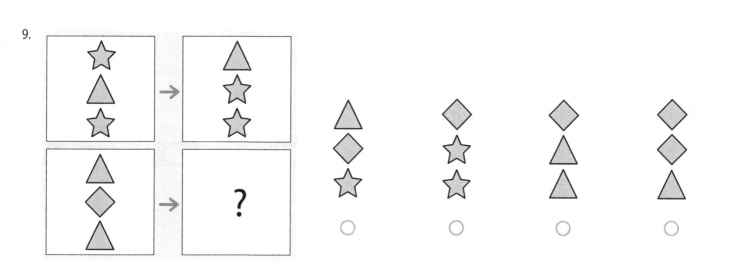

21

10.

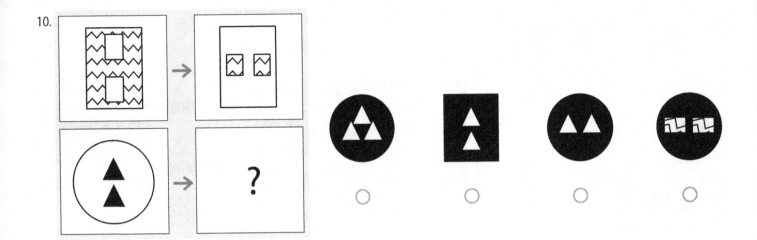

11.

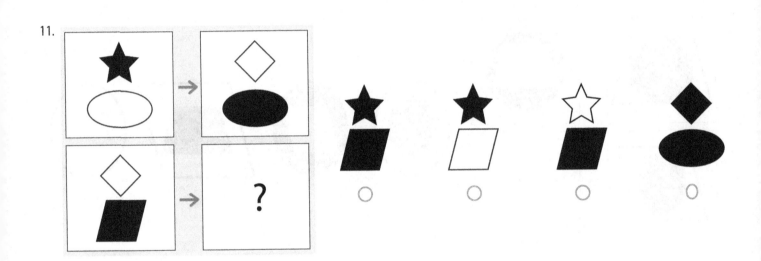

12.

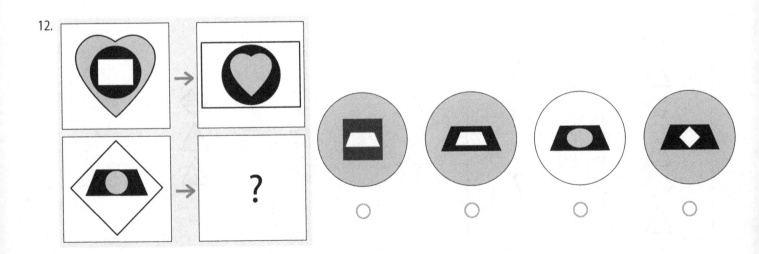

13.

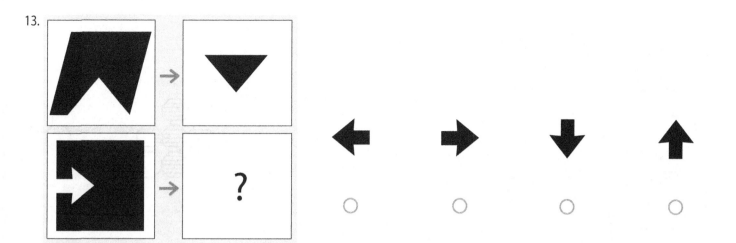

14.

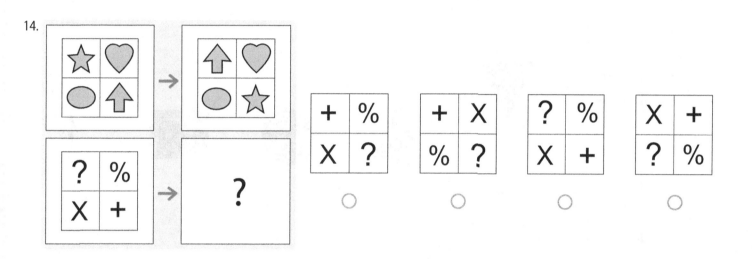

15.

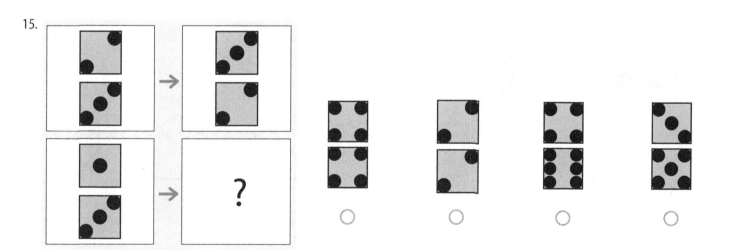

23

16.

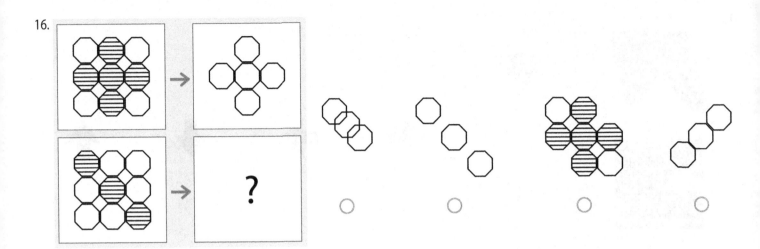

17.

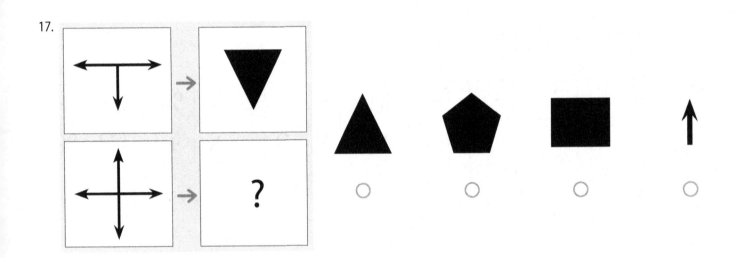

18.

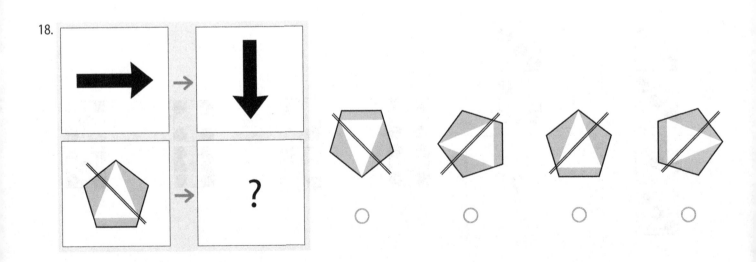

PICTURE CLASSIFICATION

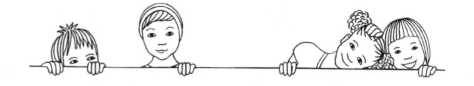

Directions (read to child):

The top row shows three pictures that are alike in some way. Look at the bottom row. There are four pictures. Which picture in the bottom row goes best with the pictures in the top row?

Explanation (for parents):

A more detailed explanation and another Picture Classification example question is on p.7. If you have not already, look over p. 7 (later). Following is an excerpt. Together with your child, try to figure out a "rule" describing how the top pictures are alike and belong together. Then, apply the "rule" to each answer choice to determine which one follows it. If your child finds that more than one choice follows the rule, then a more specific rule is needed.

Example (read to child):

Let's look at the pictures on the top row. We see a pair of boots, a pair of socks, and a high-heeled shoe. Let's come up with a "rule" to describe how these are each alike or how they belong together.

These are all things worn on your feet. Now, let's look at the bottom row. Let's find the answer choice on the bottom that follows this same rule of things that are worn on your feet. We see a glove, a hat, an ice skate, and a jacket.

Which one of these goes best with the pictures in the top row? Which one of them is worn on your feet? The ice skate.

1.

2.

3.

4.

26

5.

6.

7.

8.

9.

10.

11.

   ○   ○   ○   ○

12.

   ○   ○   ○   ○

13.

   ○   ○   ○   ○

14.

○ ○ ○ ○

15.

a   e   i

c   j   u   x

○ ○ ○ ○

16.

○ ○ ○ ○

17.

○   ○   ○   ○

18.

○   ○   ○   ○

19.

d   x   l

s   Q   i   o

○   ○   ○   ○

FIGURE CLASSIFICATION

Directions (read to child): The top row shows three pictures that are alike in some way. Look at the bottom row. There are four pictures. Which picture in the bottom row goes best with the pictures in the top row?

Explanation (for parents): A more detailed explanation of Figure Classification questions is on p.10. If you have not already, look over p. 10 (later). Following is an excerpt. Together with your child, try to figure out a "rule" describing how the top pictures are alike and belong together. Then, apply the "rule" to each answer choice to determine which one follows it. If your child finds that more than one choice follows the rule, then a more specific rule is needed.

1.

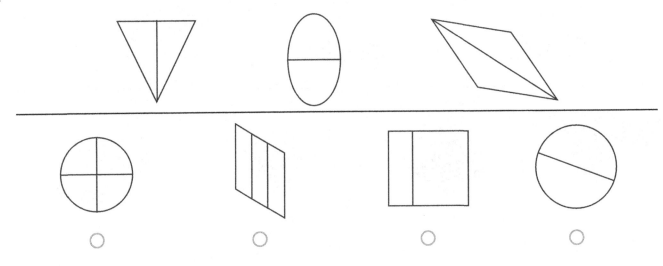

2.

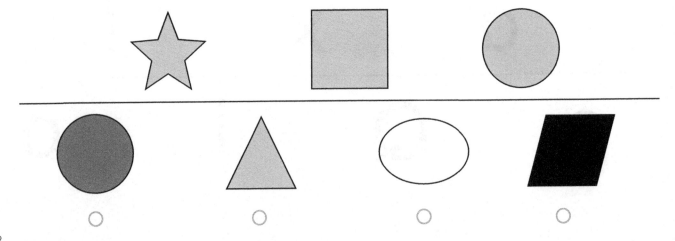

3.

4.

5.

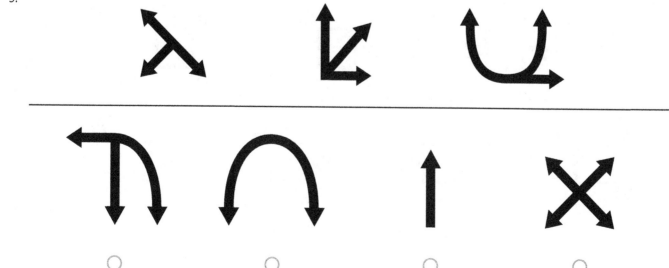

6.

  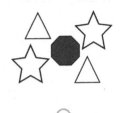

○   ○   ○   ○

7.

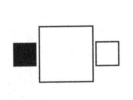 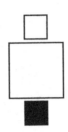 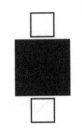

○   ○   ○   ○

8.

○   ○   ○   ○

9.

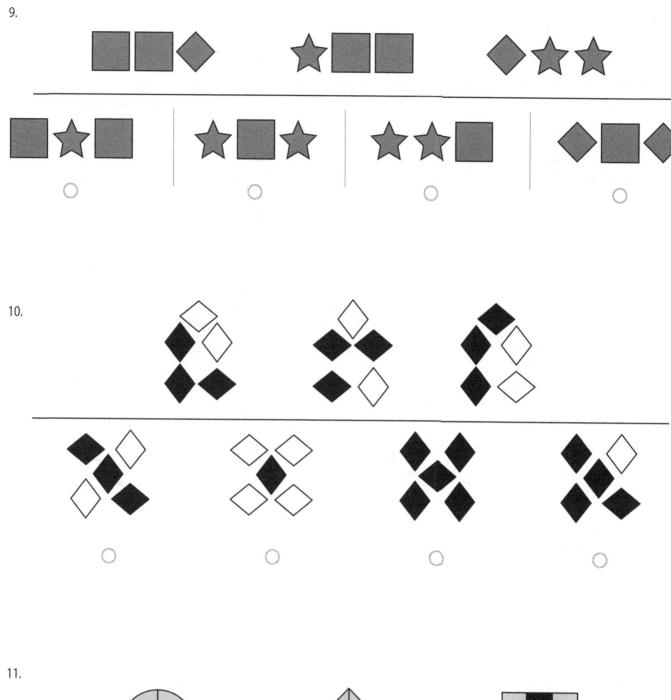

10.

11.

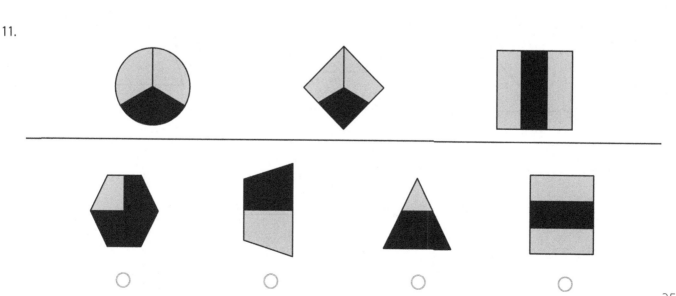

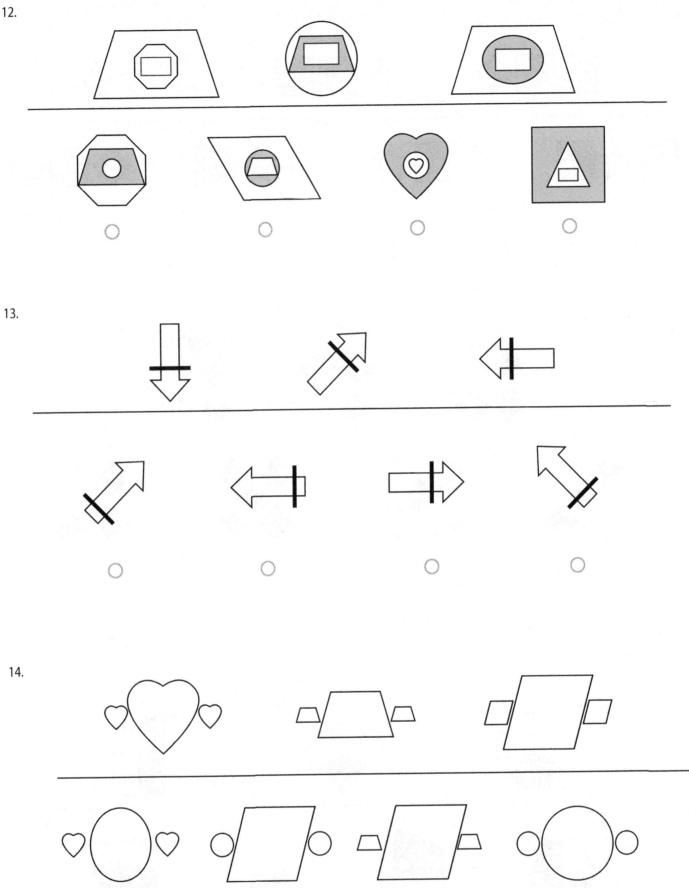

12.

13.

14.

15.

16.

17.

18.

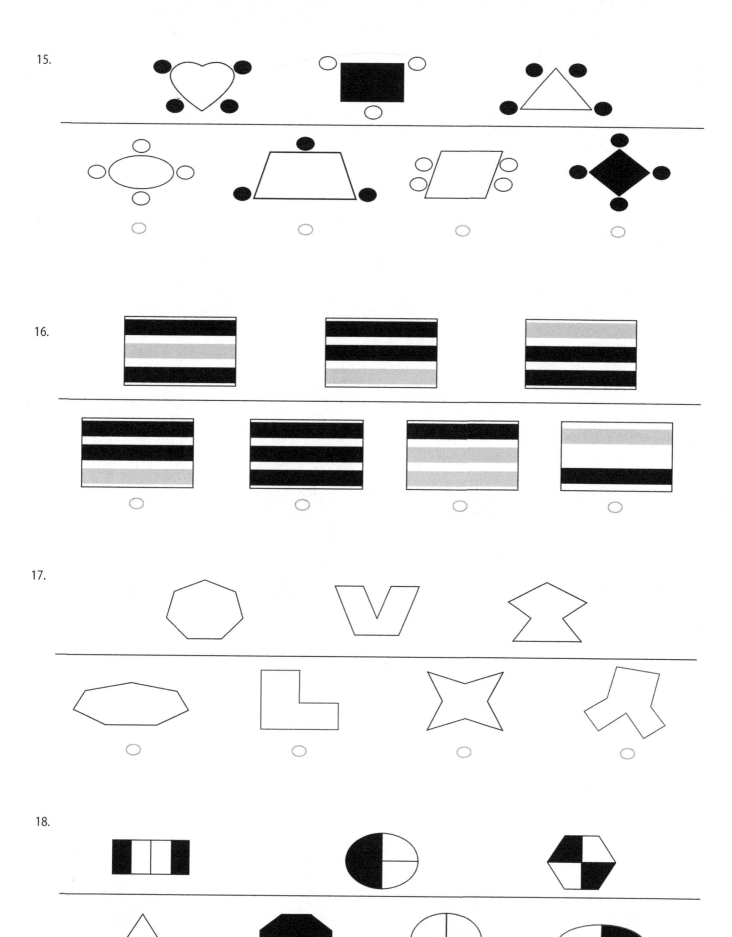

SENTENCE COMPLETION

Directions (read to child): Listen to the question, then choose the best answer. I can only read the question one time.

Additional information (for parents): Read the below questions to your child. As explained earlier in the Introduction on p.8, test administrators will read these questions only one time. Therefore, it is imperative that your child practice careful listening skills, so that you will not need to repeat the questions.

1. If you were in a doctor's office, which one of these would you most likely see?

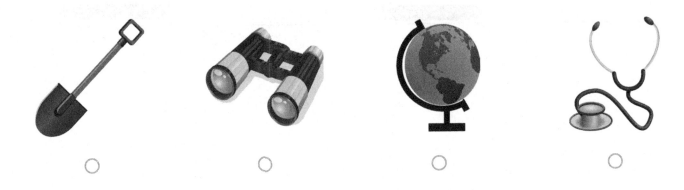

○　　　　　　　○　　　　　　　○　　　　　　　○

2. Which of these foods is not an animal product?

○　　　　　　　○　　　　　　　○　　　　　　　○

3. In science class, if you were learning about animals that experience metamorphosis, which one of these could you be learning about?

○   ○   ○   ○

4. In the shapes below, the shapes stand for different animals. A circle stands for a dog. A triangle stands for a cat. Which choice would show 1 dog and 1 cat?

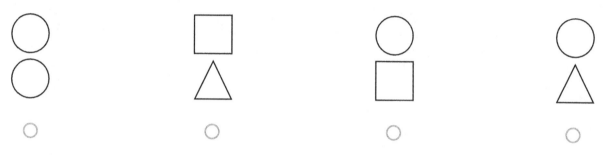

○   ○   ○   ○

5. Which of these foods would you need to peel before eating?

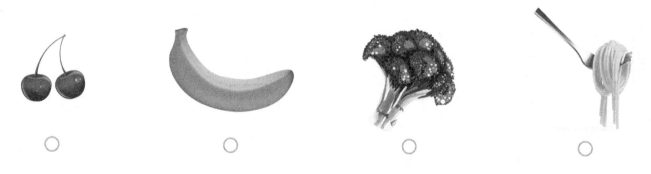

○   ○   ○   ○

6. If you needed to get somewhere rapidly, which one should you take?

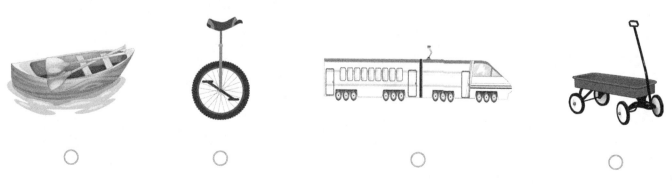

○   ○   ○   ○

7. If you were working on a science experiment in a lab, which of these would you most likely use?

8. Which choice shows a star in the middle, a heart at the end, and does not have a rectangle?

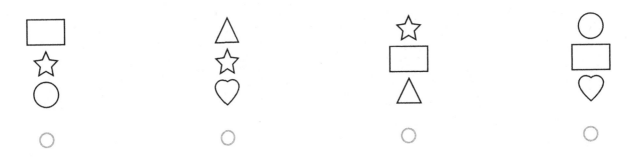

9. Which picture shows 2 shapes that are 3-D shapes?

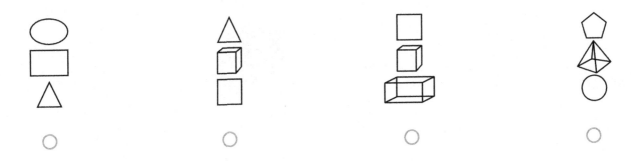

10. Which choice shows 1 living thing and 1 non-living thing?

40

11. Your friend did the following things today: painted a picture, played the piano, and helped measure the ingredients for a cake. Which choice shows all of the things your friend would have used today?

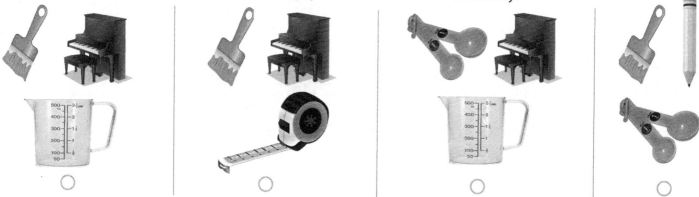

○   ○   ○   ○

12. Which choice shows 1 food picked from a tree, 1 food that grows under the ground, and 1 food caught from a boat?

○   ○   ○   ○

13. Your family did a school project together. Some of the objects you used are shown below.
Three of the different things you used were: something that measures weight, something used for heating up food, and something to protect your eyes. Which picture shows these 3 things?

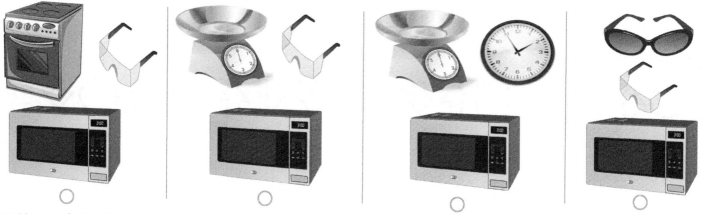

○   ○   ○   ○

14. You read a book about three animals: one animal lives in the Arctic and the other two animals live in the tropics. Which picture shows the animals that your book was about?

○   ○   ○   ○

41

15. Which one of these places would have the least precipitation?

○ ○ ○ ○

16. Which choice shows 1 animal that lives on both land and water and 1 animal that lives only in water?

   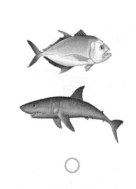

○ ○ ○ ○

17. Which shows an arrow pointing down that is to the left of an arrow pointing up?

○ ○ ○ ○

18. If you no longer had electricity, which one of these could not work?

○ ○ ○ ○

42

PAPER FOLDING

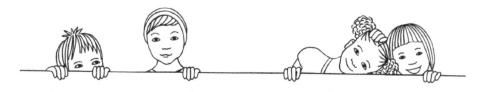

Directions (read to child): The top row of pictures shows a sheet of paper. The paper was folded, then something was cut out. Which picture in the bottom row shows how the paper would look after its unfolded?

Additional information (for parents): As explained earlier in the Introduction on p. 10, it is not uncommon for children to initially be "stumped" by Paper Folding. If your child needs help, then try demonstrating with real paper and a hole puncher. Be sure to point out the number of holes made and their position after opening the paper.

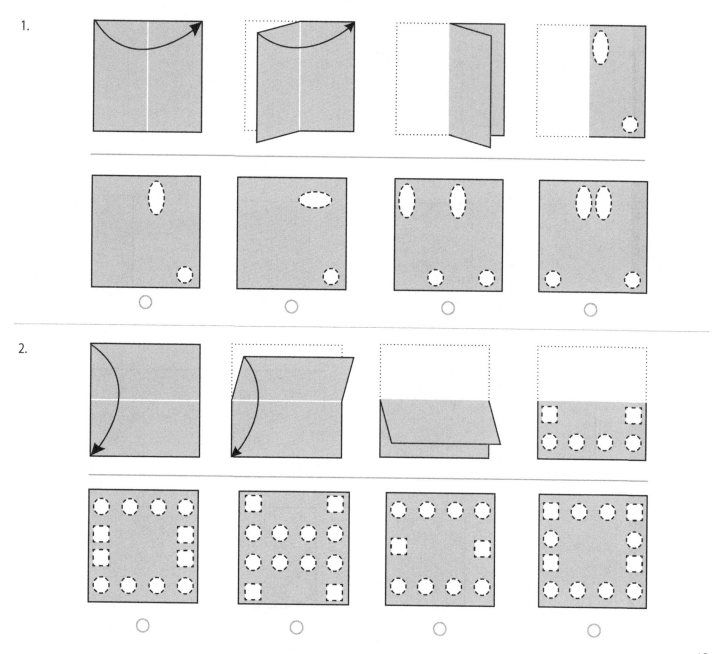

3.

○   ○   ○   ○

4.

○   ○   ○   ○

5.

○   ○   ○   ○

44

6.

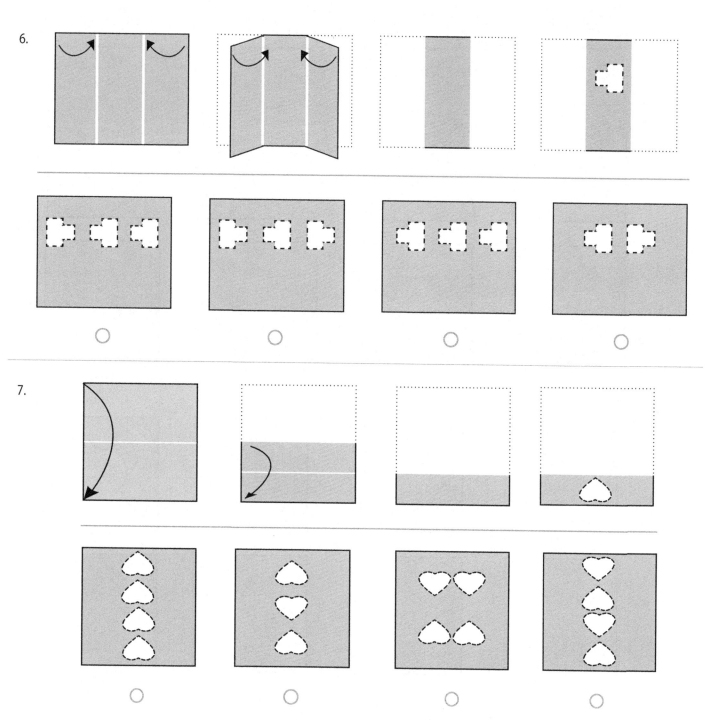

7.

8.

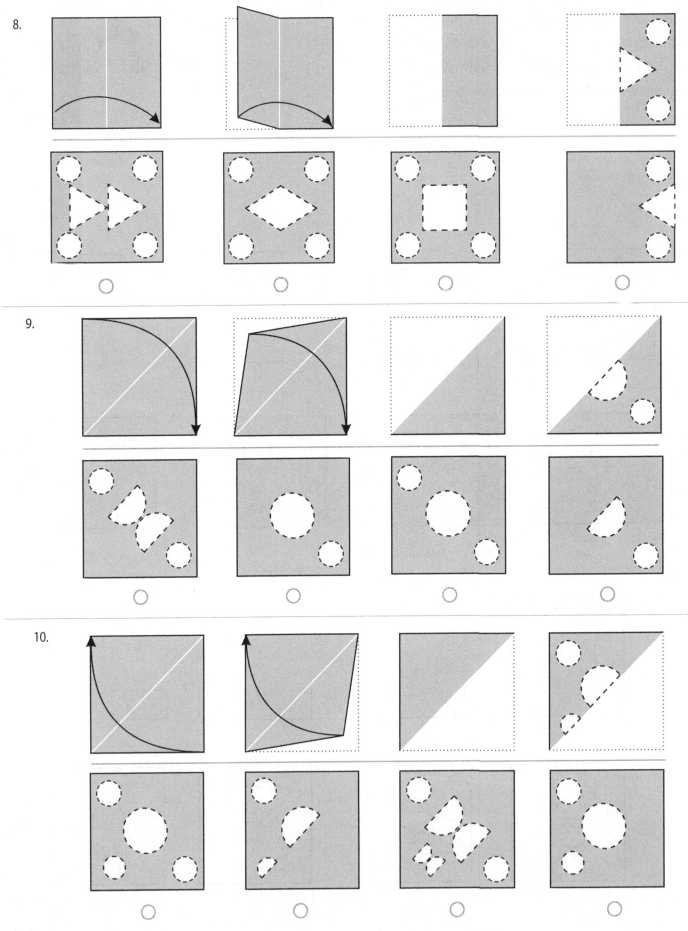

9.

10.

46

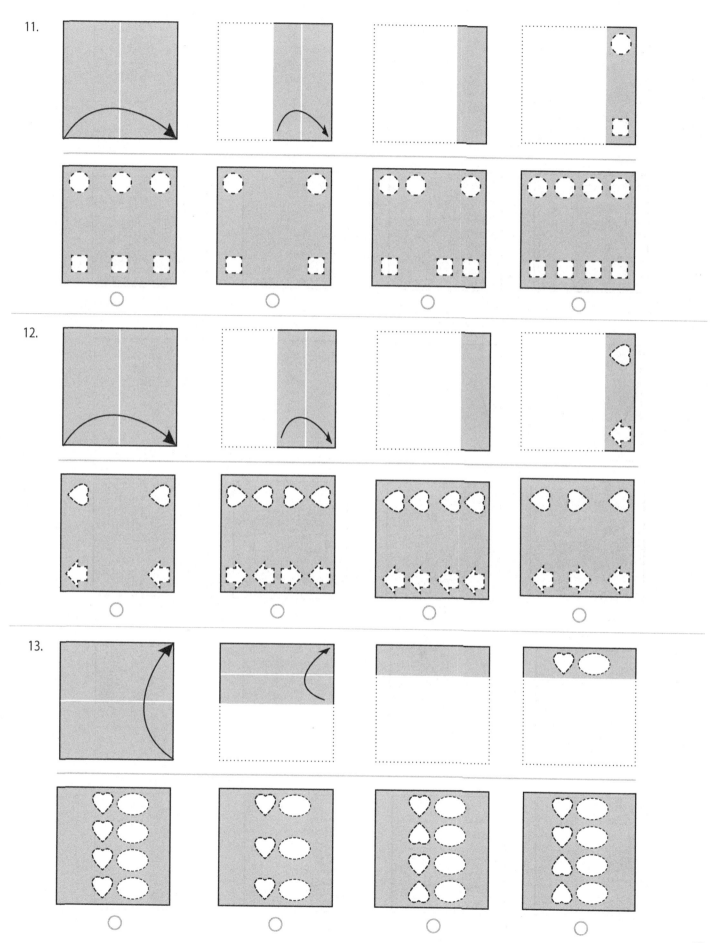

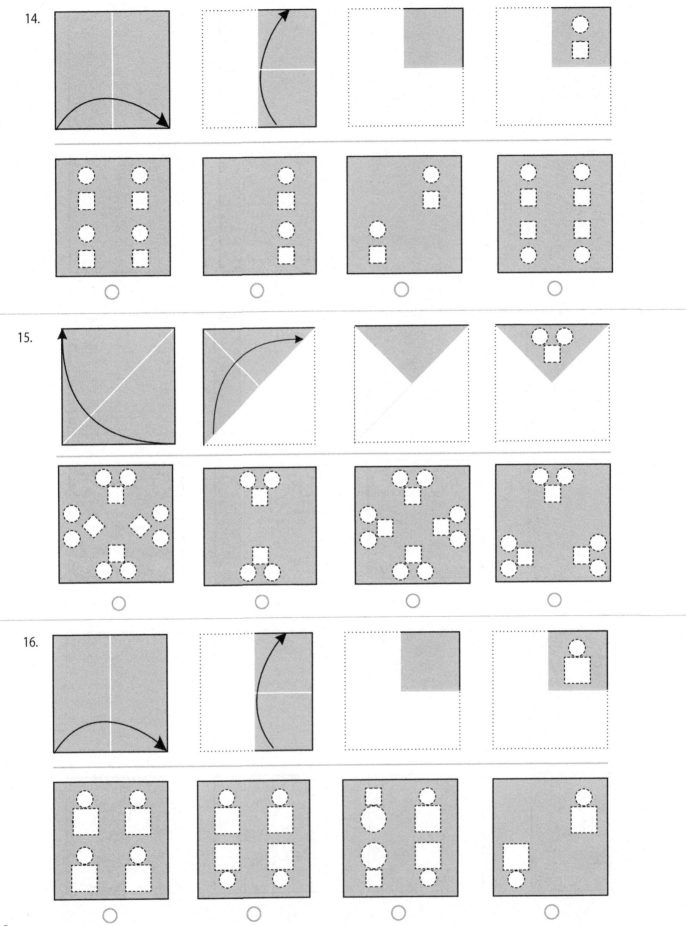

14.

15.

16.

48

NUMBER PUZZLES

Directions (read to child): Look at the box that has the question mark. Which number would go here so that both of the sides of this equal sign (point to the equal sign) have the same amount?

Additional Information: Be sure your child pays attention to the plus and minus signs. Some questions have two different signs.

You may wish to have your child circle the plus/minus signs to ensure (s)he pays attention. With multi-step equations (starting with #3), you may also want your child to write down the answer to the first part (for example, 10 (12-2 = 10), in question #3, before doing the second part (9 = 10 - ?)

1.

| 7 | = | 4 | + | ? | 4 | 3 | 2 | 1 |

                         ○   ○   ○   ○

2.

| 8 | = | 12 | - | ? | 1 | 2 | 3 | 4 |

  ○   ○   ○   ○

3.

| 9 | = | 12 | - | 2 | - | ? | 1 | 2 | 3 | 4 |

  ○   ○   ○   ○

4.

| 14 | = | 6 | + | 6 | + | ? | 0 | 1 | 2 | 3 |

  ○   ○   ○   ○

5.

| 13 | = | 9 | + | 5 | - | ? | 4 | 3 | 2 | 1 |

  ○   ○   ○   ○

6.

| 4 | = | 12 | + | 0 | - | ? | 8 | 9 | 10 | 11 |

  ○   ○   ○   ○

49

7. $9 = 10 + 6 - \,?$ 3 4 7 9 ○ ○ ○ ○

8. $4 = 7 + 6 - \,?$ 3 4 5 9 ○ ○ ○ ○

9. $5 = 9 + 3 - \,?$ 7 8 9 0 ○ ○ ○ ○

10. $1 = 8 - 3 - \,?$ 9 4 7 6 ○ ○ ○ ○

11. $8 = 17 - 12 + \,?$ 6 7 3 9 ○ ○ ○ ○

12. $4 = 8 - 3 - \,?$ 7 1 2 3 ○ ○ ○ ○

13. $19 = 9 + 2 + \,?$ 8 7 5 4 ○ ○ ○ ○

14. $18 = 14 - 5 + \,?$ 1 2 9 0 ○ ○ ○ ○

15. $5 = 17 - 8 - \,?$ 0 2 4 8 ○ ○ ○ ○

16. $1 = 3 + 2 - \,?$ 0 9 5 4 ○ ○ ○ ○

17. $0 = 12 - 4 - \,?$ 8 4 3 2 ○ ○ ○ ○

18. $9 = 17 + 1 - \,?$ 1 9 8 7 ○ ○ ○ ○

19. $5 = 4 + 2 - \,?$ 1 2 3 4 ○ ○ ○ ○

20. $8 = 11 + 3 - \,?$ 0 5 6 7 ○ ○ ○ ○

21. $14 = 13 - 2 + \,?$ 1 2 3 4 ○ ○ ○ ○

22. $9 = 15 - 6 + \,?$ 12 3 9 0 ○ ○ ○ ○

NUMBER SERIES

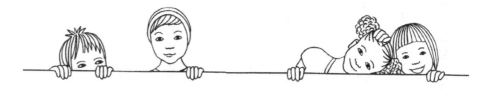

Directions (read to child): Which rod should go in the place of the missing rod to finish the pattern?

Explanation (for parents): The final rod of the abacus is missing. Before this missing rod, the rods of the abacus have made a pattern. Your child must look closely to determine the pattern, as the more challenging Number Series questions are quite difficult. Be sure your child correctly counts the number of beads on each rod.

Note that some rods do not have any beads. Rods without any beads equal "0". The gray line appears above the 5th bead's place.

Example (read to child): Let's look at this picture on the left. It shows an abacus. The abacus has rods going bottom to top. On these rods are beads. These rods have made a pattern that we need to figure out.

First, we see a rod without any beads. This rod equals "0". After this rod with zero beads, then we see 1 bead, 2 beads, 3 beads, 4 beads, and finally the missing rod. What is the pattern that these rods have made? Each rod has one more bead than the rod before it.

If this is the pattern, what should the next rod be (the rod that would go in place of the missing rod on the abacus)? The rod with 5 beads, choice B.

1.

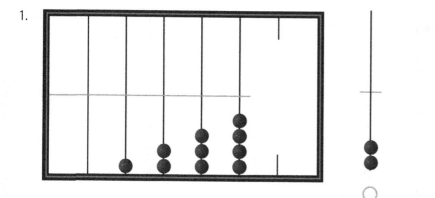   

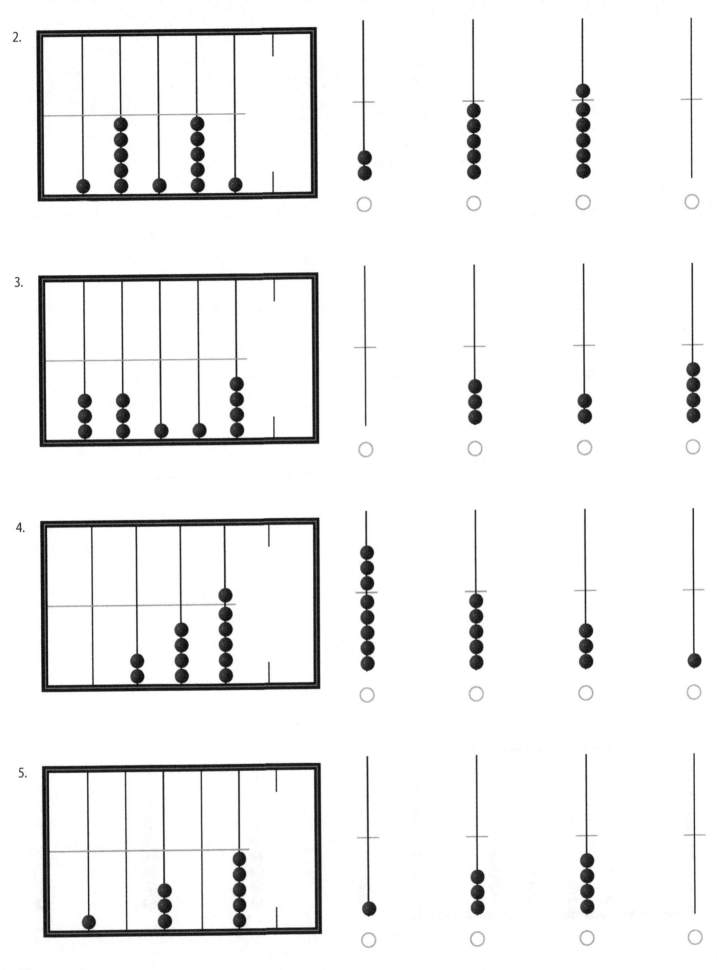

52

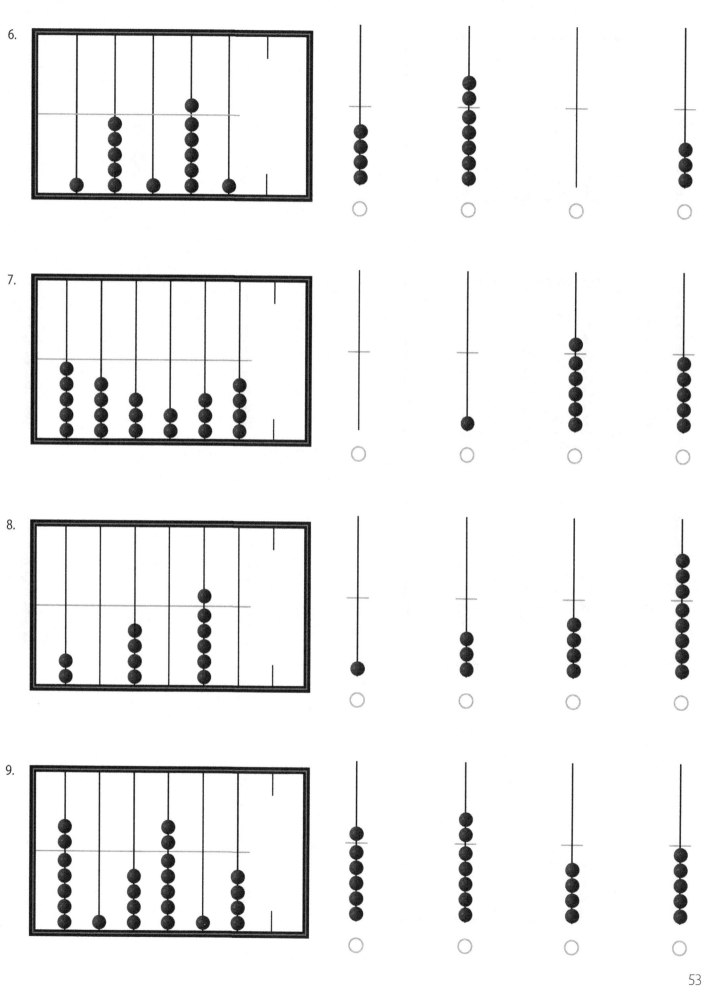

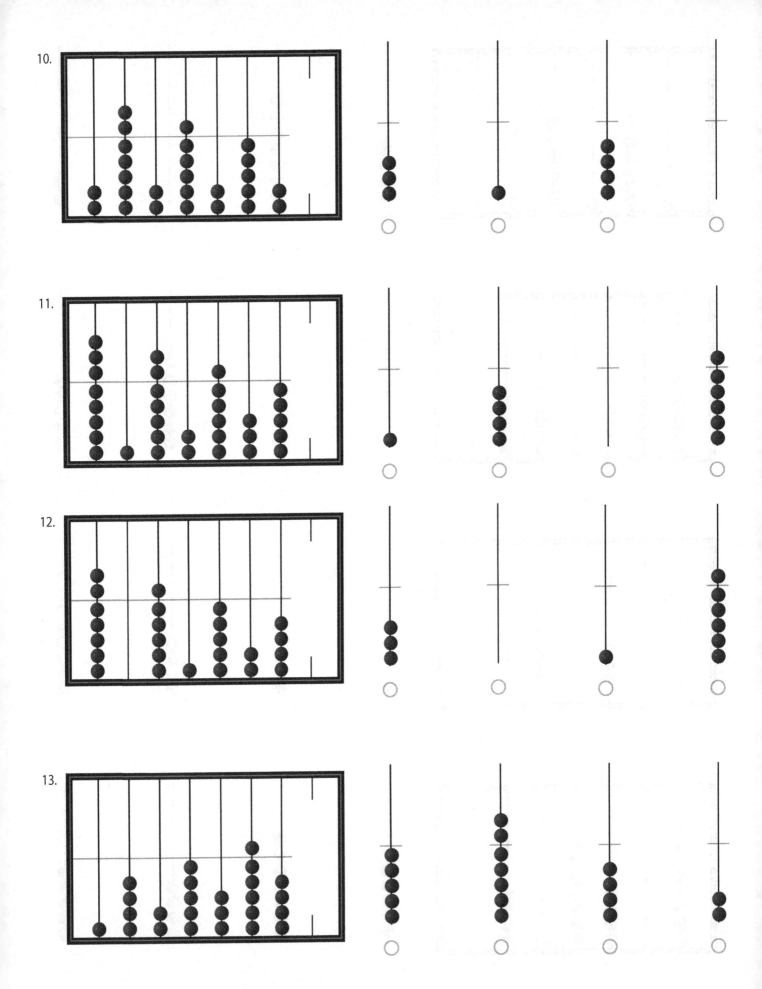

54

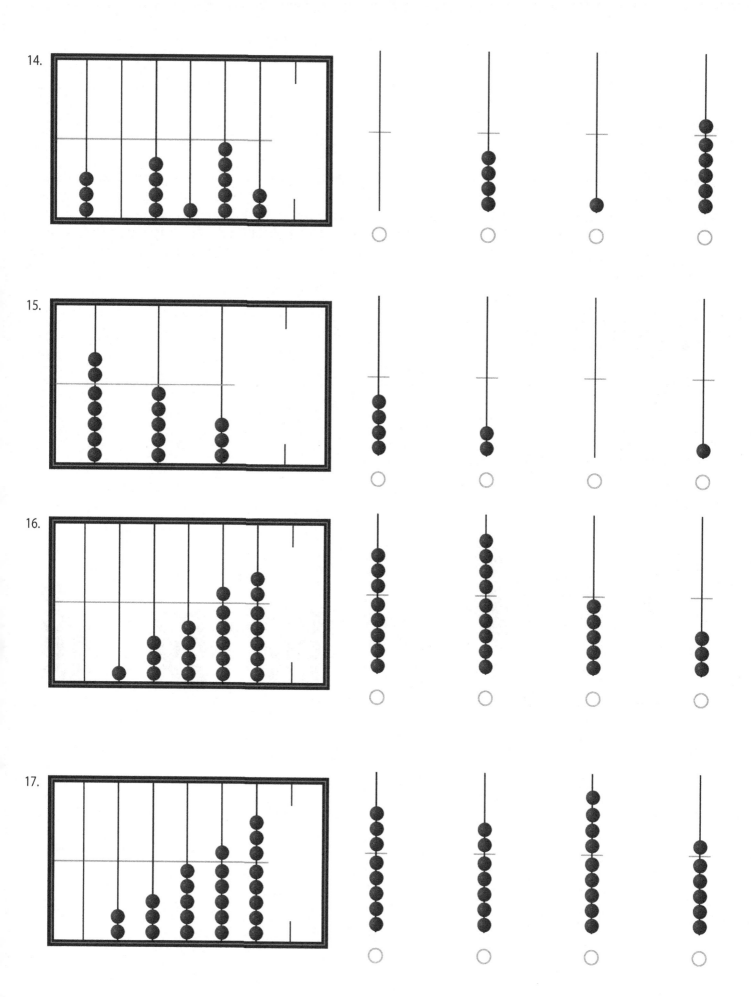

NUMBER ANALOGIES

Directions (read to child): The pictures in the top boxes go together in some way. Look at the bottom boxes. One box is empty. Which answer choice goes with the picture in the bottom box like the pictures in the top boxes do?

Explanation (for parents): A more detailed explanation and example questions are on p. 11. Look over p.11 (later), if you have not already. Your child must figure out how the images in top set of boxes are related mathematically. Then, (s)he must figure out which answer choice would go with the bottom left image so that the bottom set would have the same relationship. For example, the mathematical relationship in the first question is "minus five". After counting the objects in the boxes, you may want your child to write the number by the box, so (s)he does not forget the quantity.

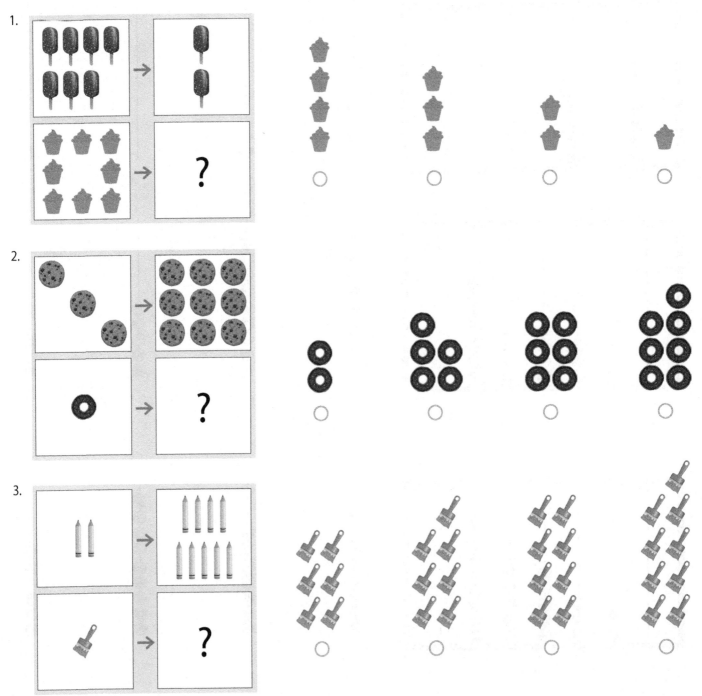

56

4.

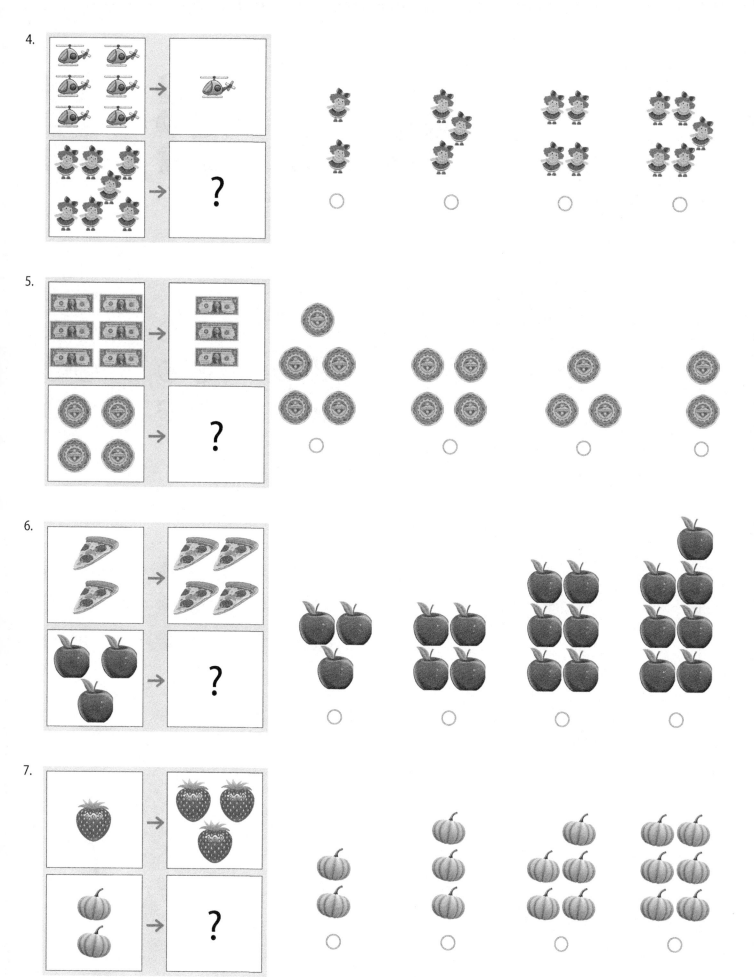

5.

6.

7.

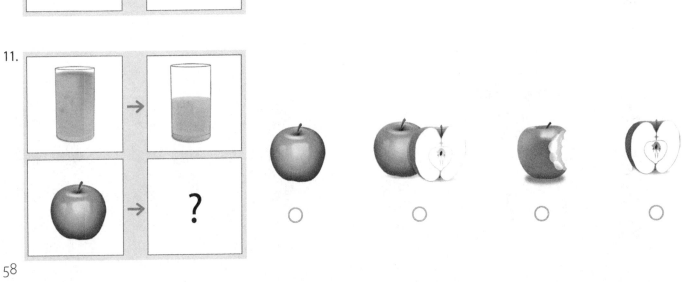

58

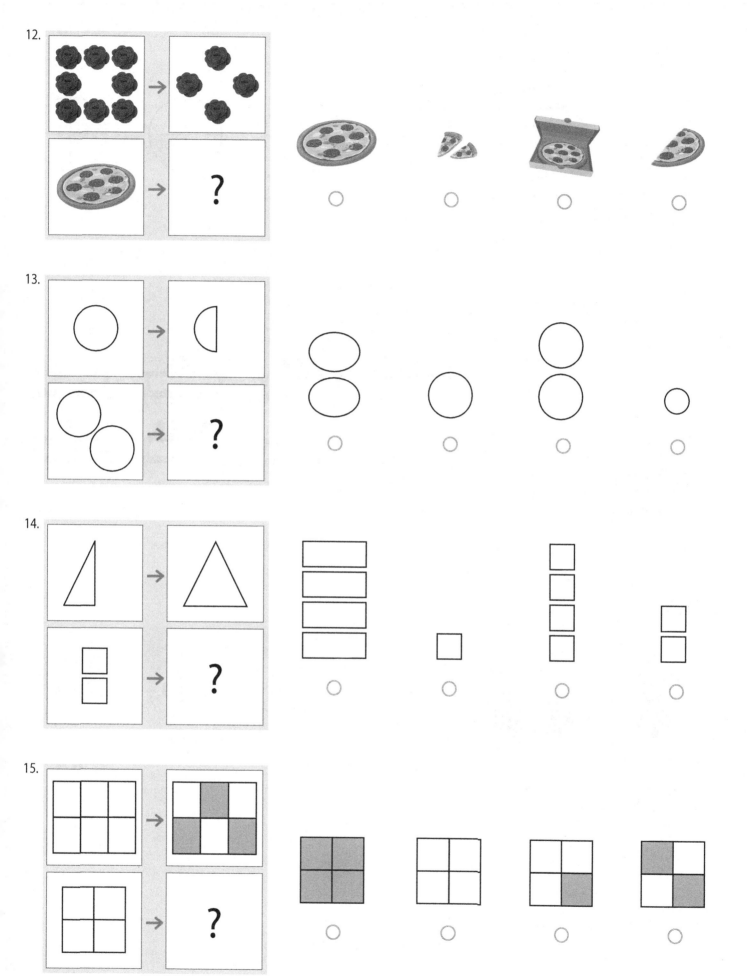

12.

13.

14.

15.

59

16.

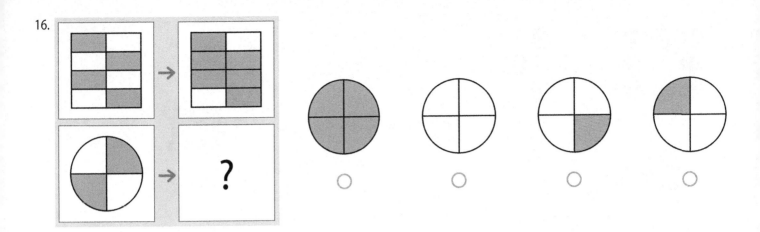

17.

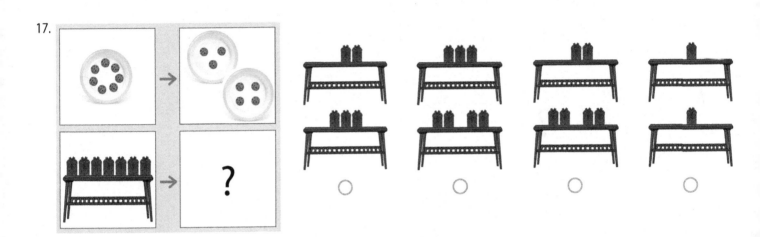

18.

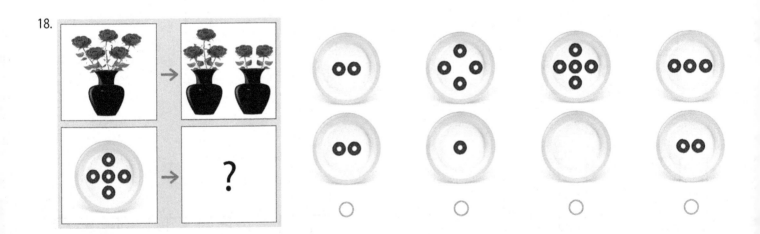

- End of Practice Test 1. -

- Practice Test 2 begins on the next page. -

START OF PRACTICE TEST 2 / PICTURE ANALOGIES

Directions: The pictures on top go together in some way. Look at the bottom boxes. One is empty. Look at the answer choices. Which one goes with the picture in the bottom box in the same way the top pictures go together?

1.

2.

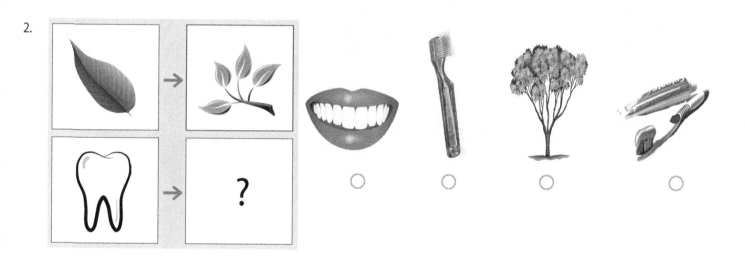

3.

4.

5.

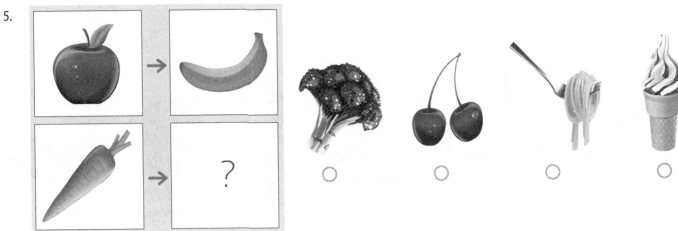

6.

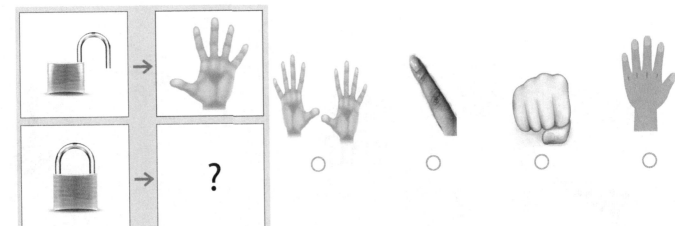

62

7.

8.

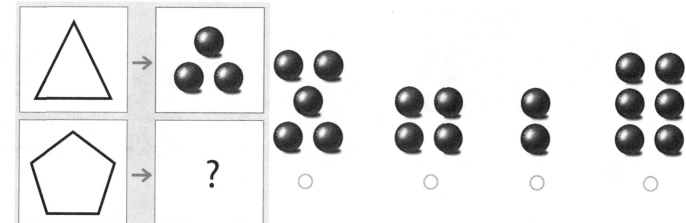

9.

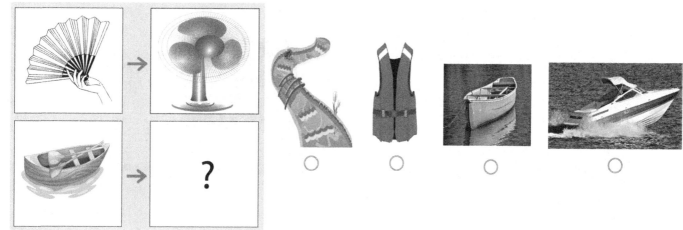

63

10.

11.

12.

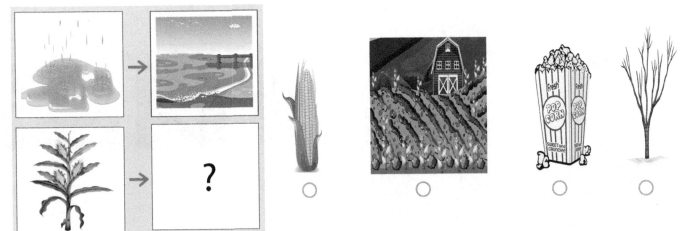

64

13.

14.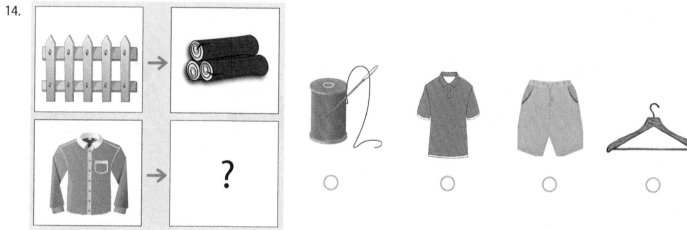

15.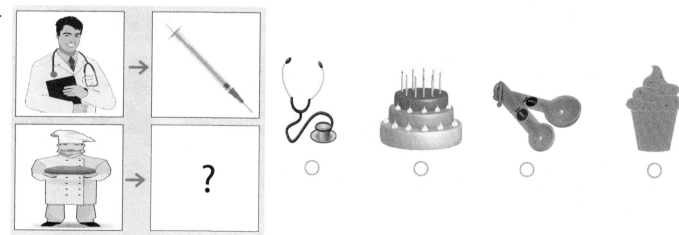

65

16.

17.

18.

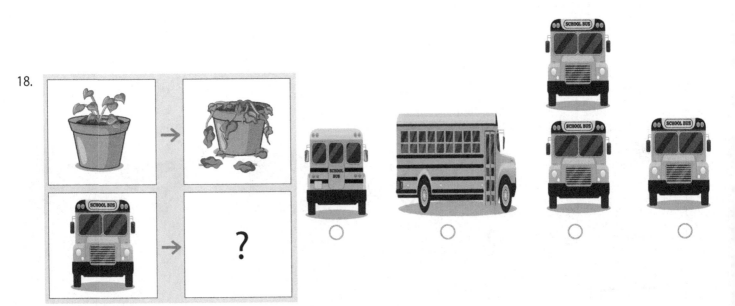

PICTURE CLASSIFICATION

Directions: The top row shows three pictures that are alike in some way. Look at the bottom row. There are four pictures. Which picture in the bottom row goes best with the pictures in the top row?

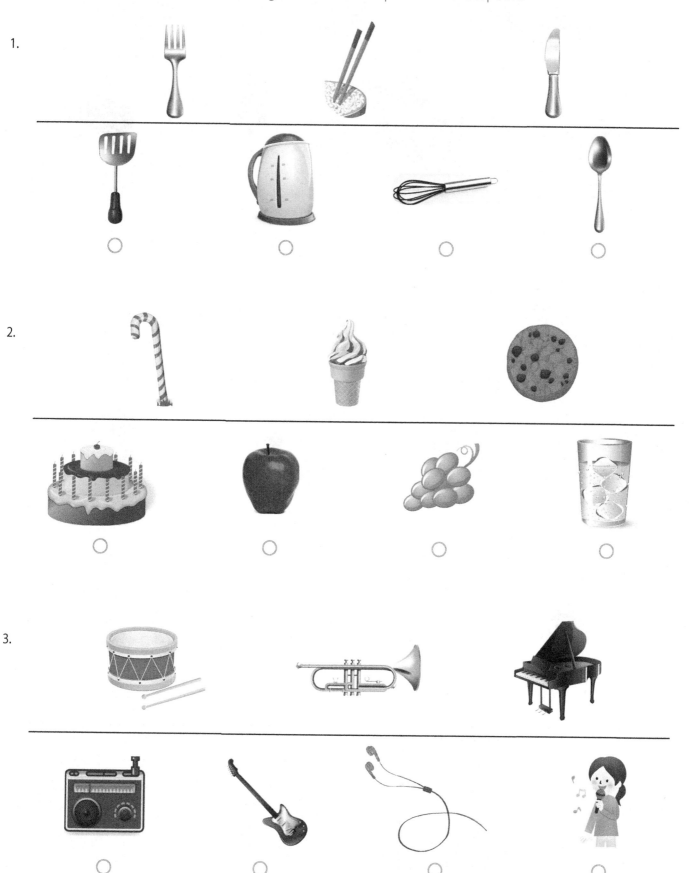

1.

2.

3.

4.

○ ○ ○ ○

5.

  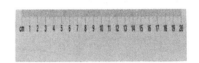

○ ○ ○ ○

6.

○ ○ ○ ○

7.

○ ○ ○ ○

8.

○ ○ ○ ○

9.

 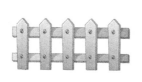  

○ ○ ○ ○

10.

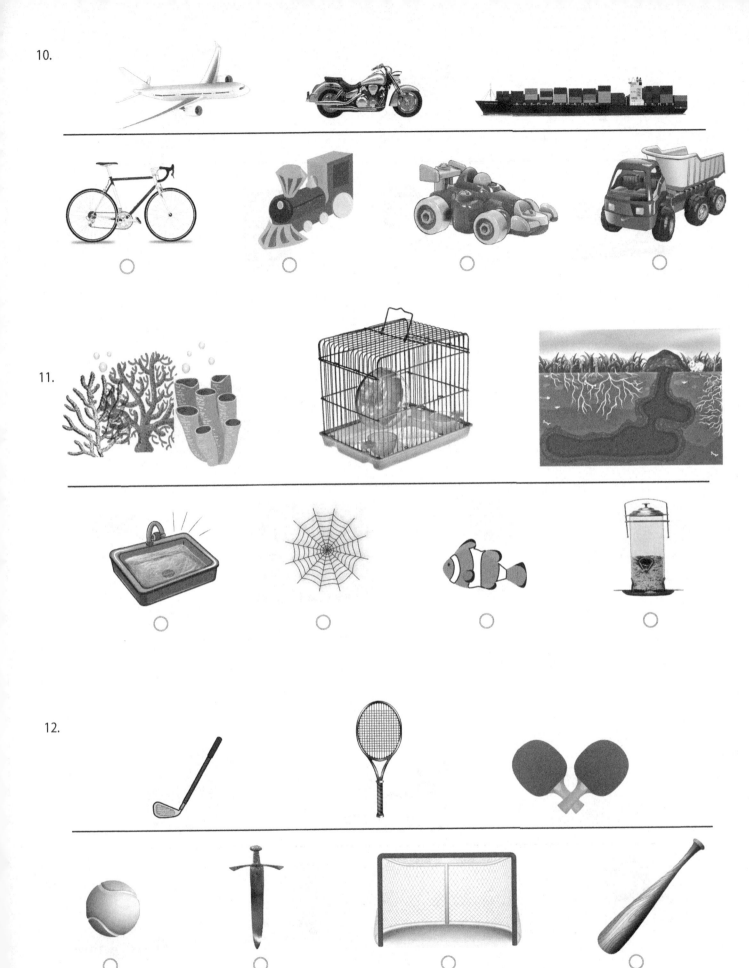

11.

12.

70

13.

M   W   V

t   I   N   U

○   ○   ○   ○

14.

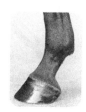  

○   ○   ○   ○

15.

○   ○   ○   ○

16.

17.

18.

SENTENCE COMPLETION

1. There are three things in your backpack: a calculator, a notebook, and a box of crayons. Which picture shows something that is not in your backpack?

○   ○   ○   ○

2. Which choice shows a picture of an animal that would have the least number of legs?

○   ○   ○   ○

3. Which picture shows only animals you would usually find in the jungle?

○   ○   ○   ○

4. Which picture only shows things that are worn in pairs?

○   ○   ○   ○

73

5. Your teacher tells you that you are going to learn about something ancient. Which one of these are you most likely going to learn about?

○   ○   ○   ○

6. In the shapes below, the shapes stand for different foods. A square stands for bread. A triangle stands for cheese. A circle stands for an apple. Which picture would show bread, cheese, apple?

○   ○   ○   ○

7. Which picture shows 1 food grown under the ground, 1 food grown on a vine, and 1 food grown on trees?

○   ○   ○   ○

8. Which one shows something that is not used to measure time?

○   ○   ○   ○

9. Your friend has 3 favorite animals – 1 is a reptile and 2 are mammals. Which picture shows your friend's 3 favorite animals?

○   ○   ○   ○

10. Which choice has a circle in between a rectangle and a triangle, where the triangle is to the right of a circle?

○   ○   ○   ○

11. You have to write a paragraph about 2 animals – one animal that hibernates and one animal that migrates in winter. Which choice shows two animals that your paragraph could be about?

○   ○   ○   ○

12. Which picture shows three things found in trees and one thing found in water?

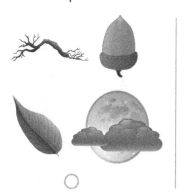         

○   ○   ○   ○

13. Which picture shows this: A cookie is below the drink. A cupcake is above the spoon. The drink is between the cookie and the spoon?

14. Which picture shows one animal that is extinct and one that still exists?

15. Which picture shows four shapes that are 3-D shapes?

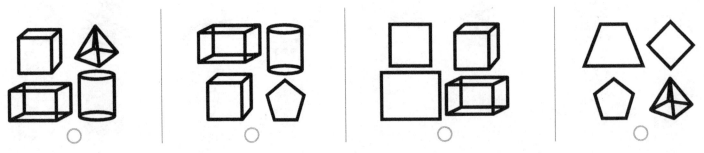

16. Which choice has the number 1 between the number 3 and the number 4, where the number 4 is to the right of the number 1?

8341   3148   4183   1438

○   ○   ○   ○

17. After school today, your friend did three different things. Your friend played two musical instruments and played one sport. Which picture shows the three things she would have used?

○   ○   ○   ○

18. Look at the shapes below. A circle stands for a cake. A diamond stands for a cookie. A heart stands for a balloon. Which picture shows, in this order: cake, cookie, balloon?

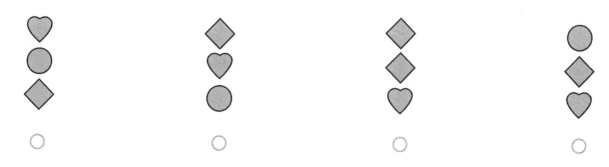

○   ○   ○   ○

FIGURE ANALOGIES

Directions: The pictures on top go together in some way. Look at the bottom boxes. One is empty. Look at the row of answer choices. Which one goes with the picture in the bottom box like the pictures on top go together?

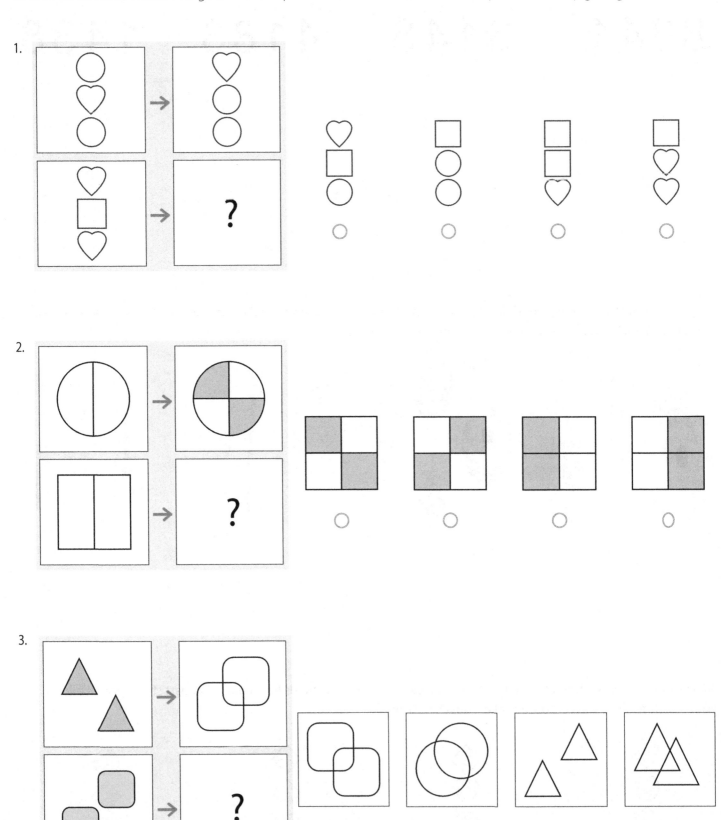

1.

2.

3.

4.

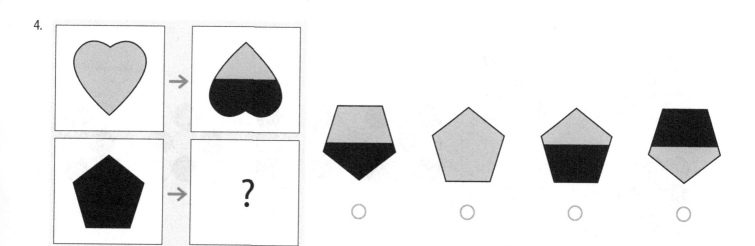

5.

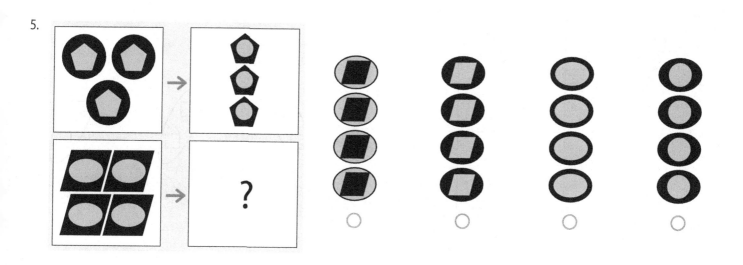

6.

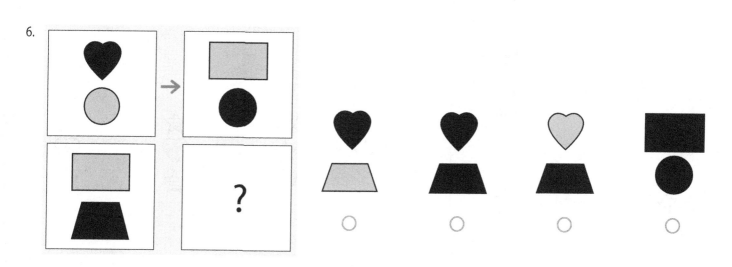

7.

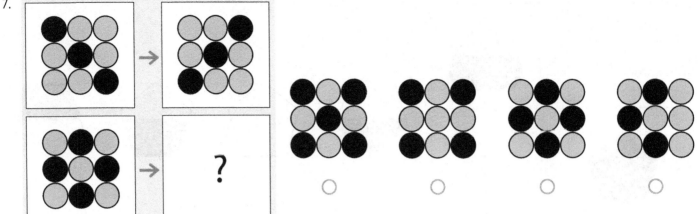

8.

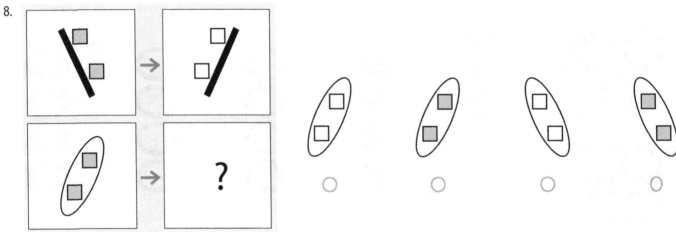

9.

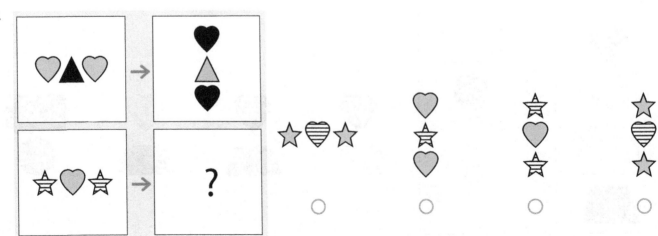

10.

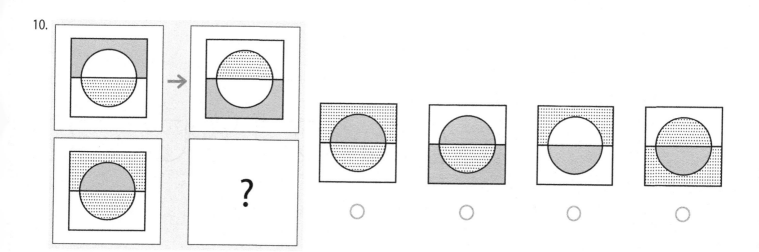

11.

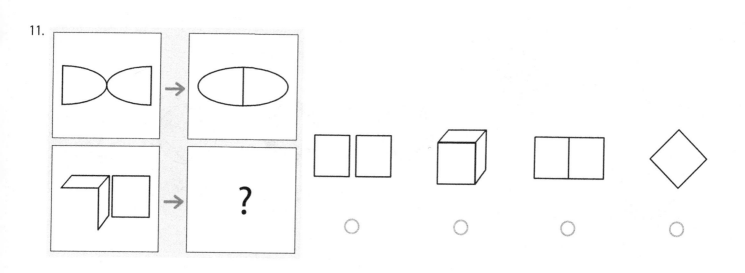

12.

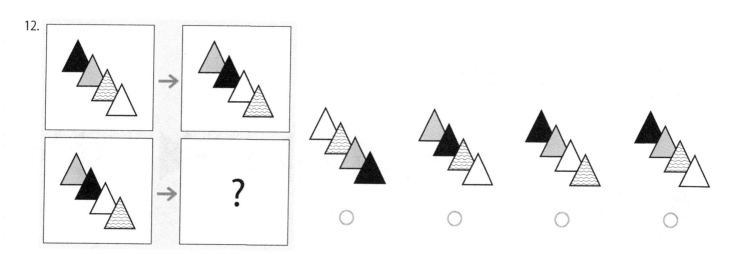

13.

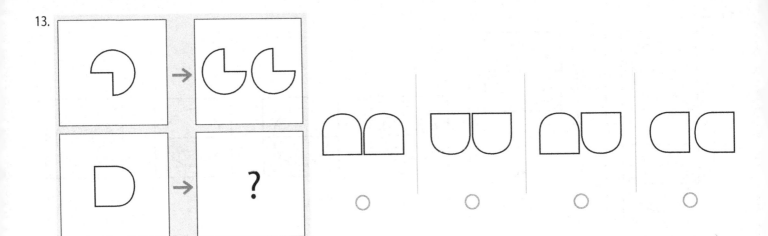

○ ○ ○ ○

14.

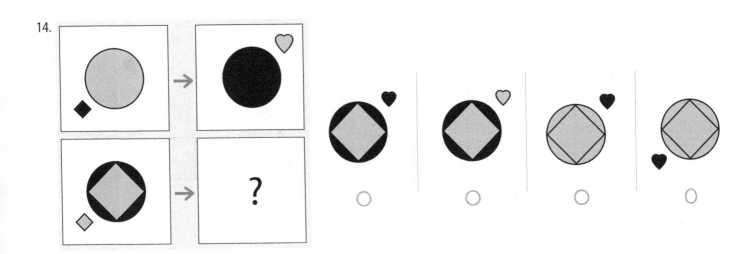

○ ○ ○ ○

15.

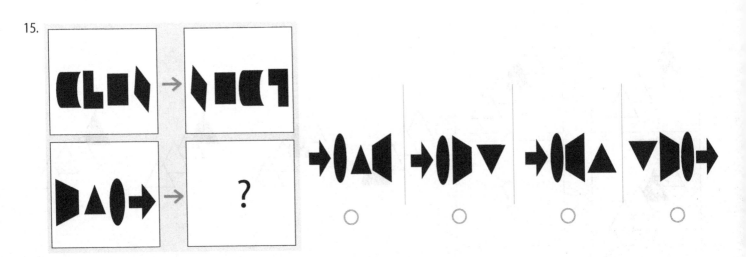

○ ○ ○ ○

16.

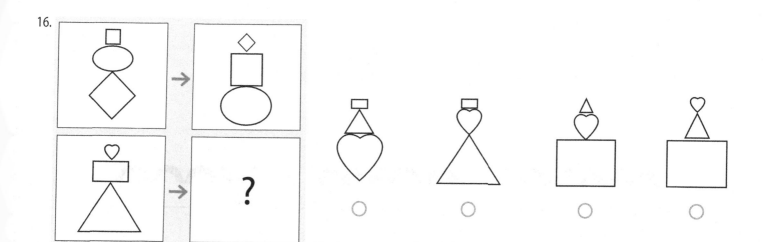

17.

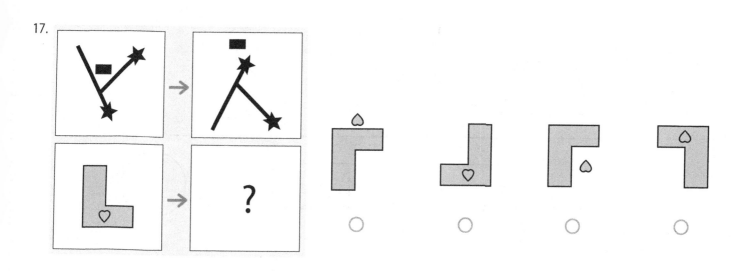

18.

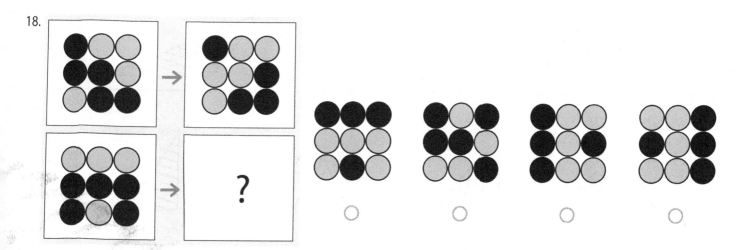

FIGURE CLASSIFICATION

Directions: The top row shows three pictures that are alike in some way. Look at the bottom row. There are four pictures. Which picture in the bottom row goes best with the pictures in the top row?

1.

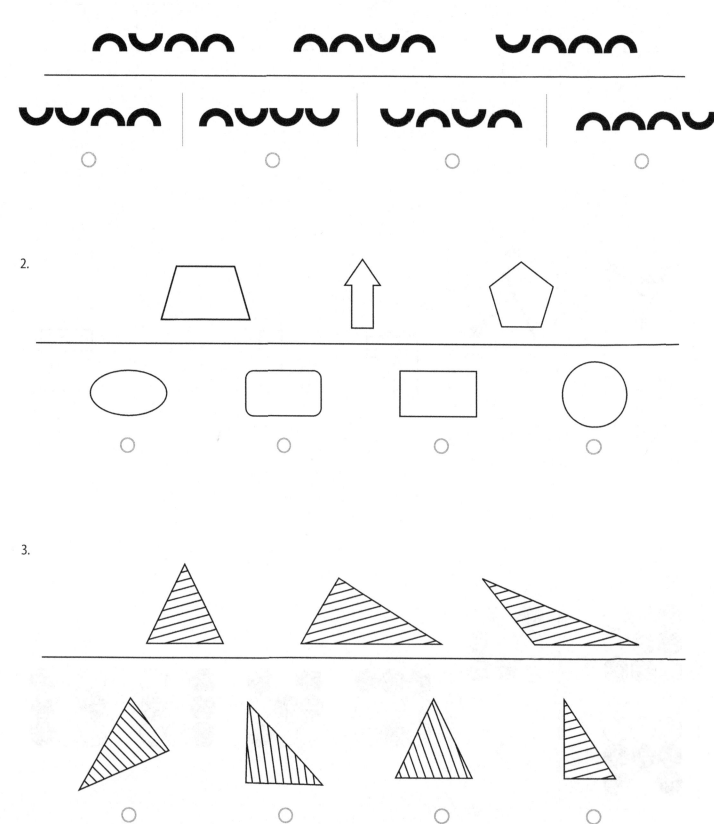

2.

3.

4.

 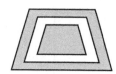

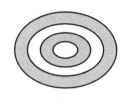 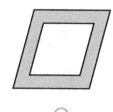  

○ ○ ○ ○

5.

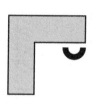

  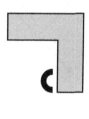 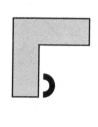

○ ○ ○ ○

6.

○ ○ ○ ○

7.

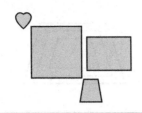 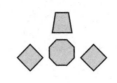 

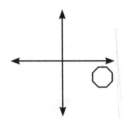 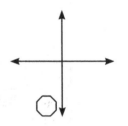

○ ○ ○ ○

8.

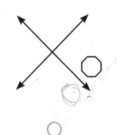  

○ ○ ○ ○

9.

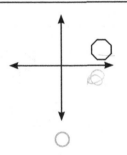

   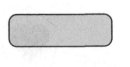

○ ○ ○ ○

10.

11.

12.

13.

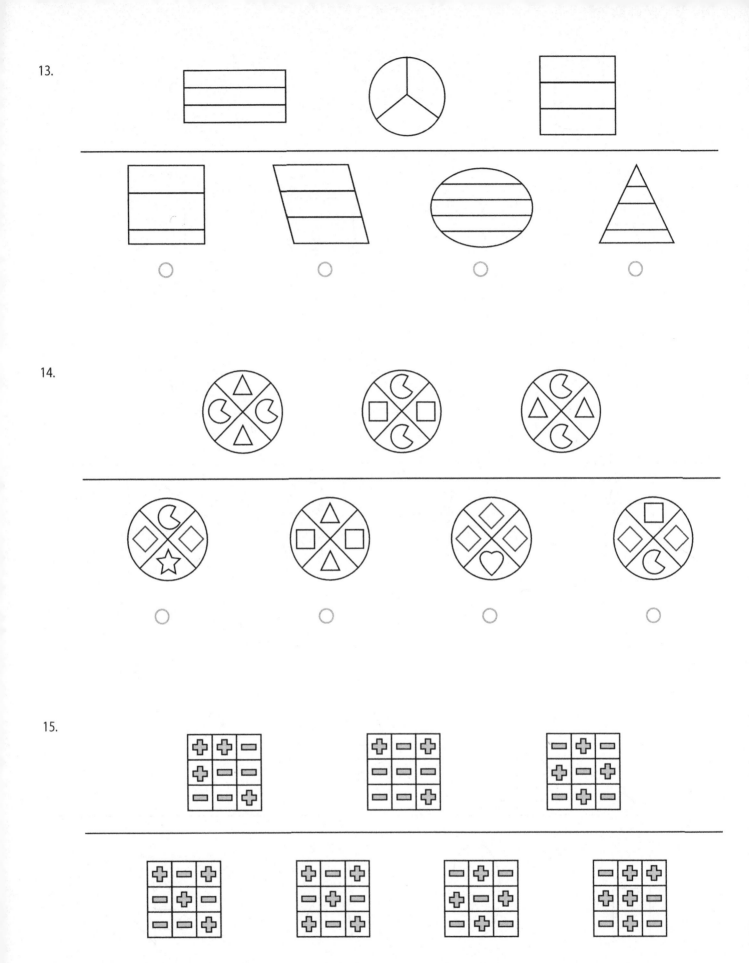

14.

15.

16.

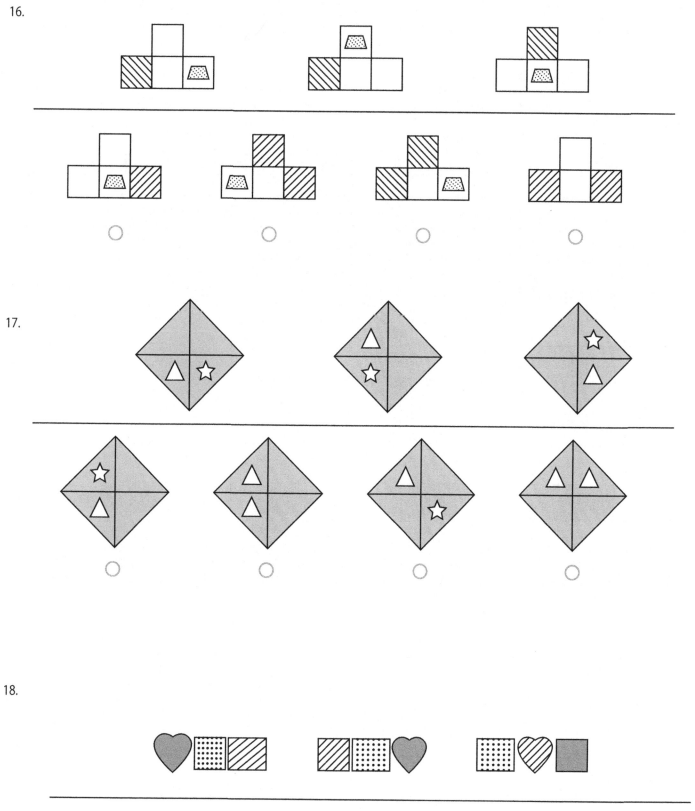

17.

18.

PAPER FOLDING

Directions: The top row of pictures show a sheet of paper, how it was folded, and how something was cut out. Which picture in the bottom row shows how the paper would look after its unfolded?

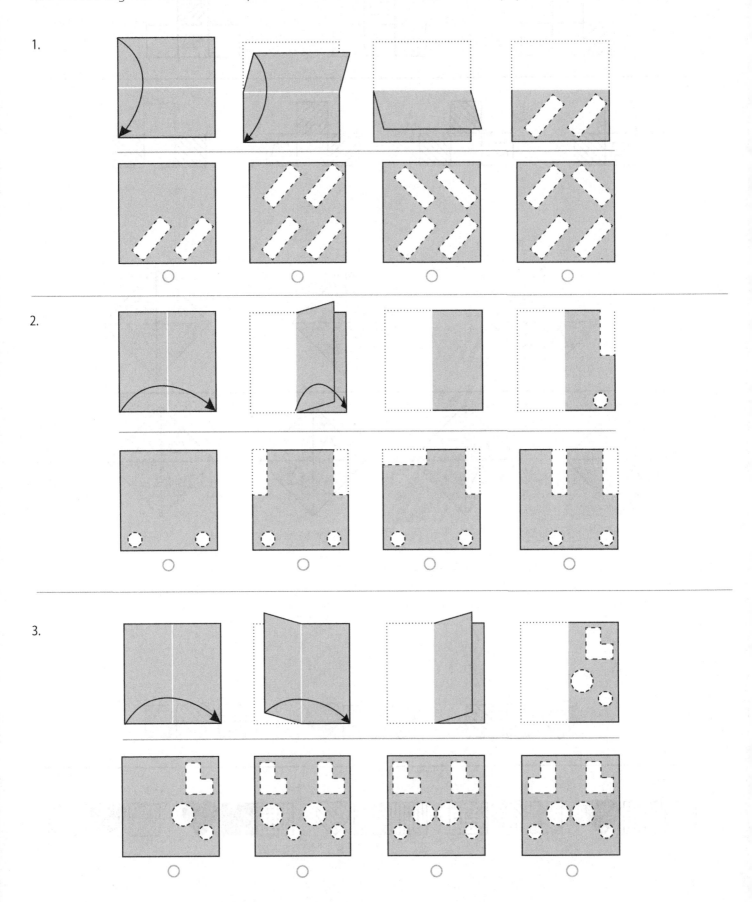

1.

2.

3.

4.

5.

6.

7.

○   ○   ○   ○

8.

○   ○   ○   ○

9.

○   ○   ○   ○

10..

11.

12.

13..

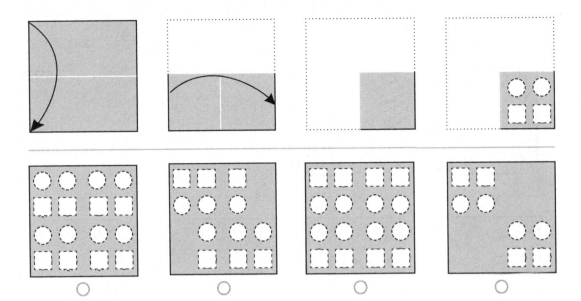

○ ○ ○ ○

14.

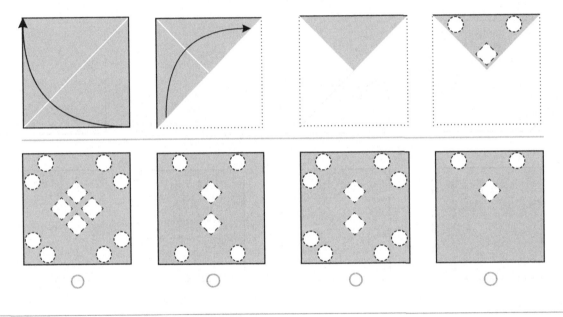

○ ○ ○ ○

15.

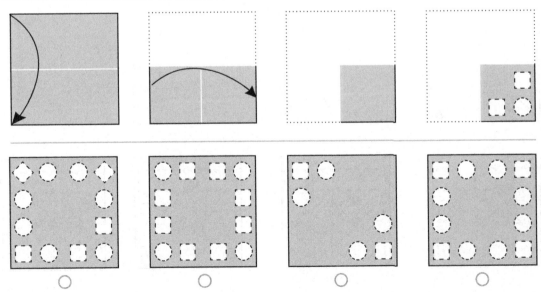

○ ○ ○ ○

94

NUMBER PUZZLES

Directions: Which number would go in place of the box with the question mark so that both of the sides of this equal sign have the same amount?

1.

$11 = 14 + 3 - ?$

0 ○ 1 ○ 6 ○ 17 ○

2.

$9 = 18 - 6 - ?$

3 ○ 4 ○ 5 ○ 6 ○

3.

$19 = 7 + 1 + ?$

10 ○ 13 ○ 12 ○ 11 ○

4.

$18 = 0 + 18 - ?$

0 ○ 1 ○ 2 ○ 3 ○

5.

$2 = 14 + 3 - ?$

14 ○ 15 ○ 9 ○ 13 ○

6.

$11 = 6 - 4 + ?$

1 ○ 9 ○ 10 ○ 11 ○

7.

$14 = 19 + 3 - ?$

2 ○   11 ○   10 ○   8 ○

8.

$0 = 11 + 8 - ?$

19 ○   3 ○   4 ○   18 ○

9.

$10 = 5 - 4 + ?$

3 ○   2 ○   9 ○   1 ○

10.

$17 = 6 - 2 + ?$

11 ○   13 ○   9 ○   12 ○

11.

$18 = 8 - 0 + ?$

10 ○   8 ○   6 ○   18 ○

12.

$4 = 11 + 2 - ?$

5 ○   4 ○   13 ○   9 ○

13.

$1 = 5 + 11 - \boxed{?}$

15 ○ 16 ○ 17 ○ 18 ○

14.

$15 = 0 + 12 + \boxed{?}$

12 ○ 4 ○ 3 ○ 15 ○

15.

$9 = 13 - 3 - \boxed{?}$

10 ○ 1 ○ 0 ○ 7 ○

16.

$13 = 14 - 9 + \boxed{?}$

5 ○ 12 ○ 10 ○ 8 ○

17.

$18 = 15 - 8 + \boxed{?}$

11 ○ 7 ○ 5 ○ 13 ○

18.

$3 = 19 - 7 - \boxed{?}$

12 ○ 13 ○ 9 ○ 8 ○

NUMBER ANALOGIES

Directions: The pictures on top go together in some way. One of the bottom boxes is empty. Which answer choice would make the bottom boxes go together like the top pictures do?

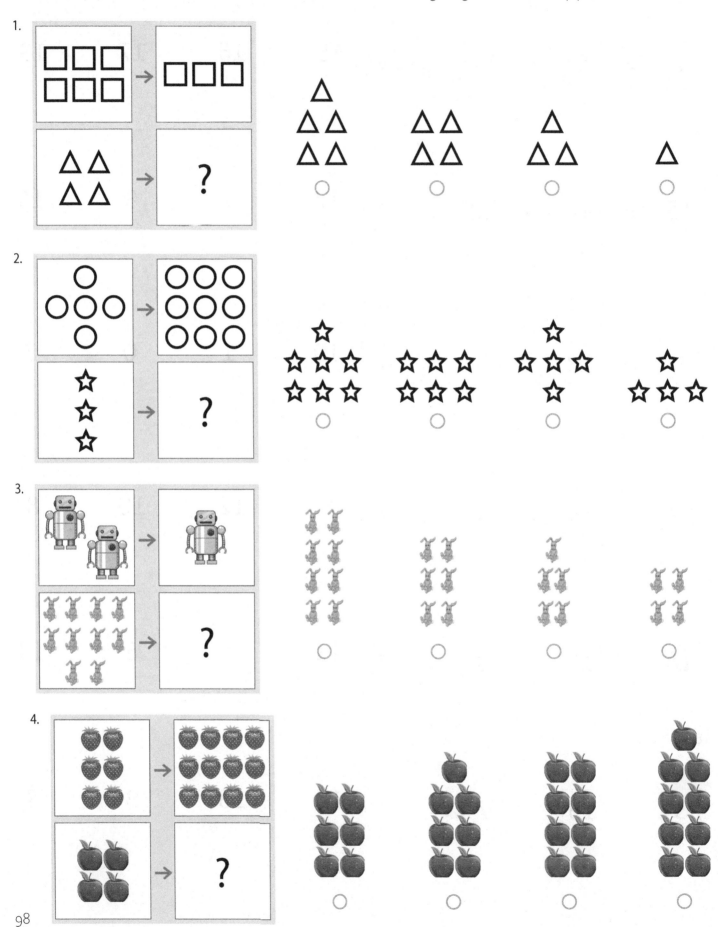

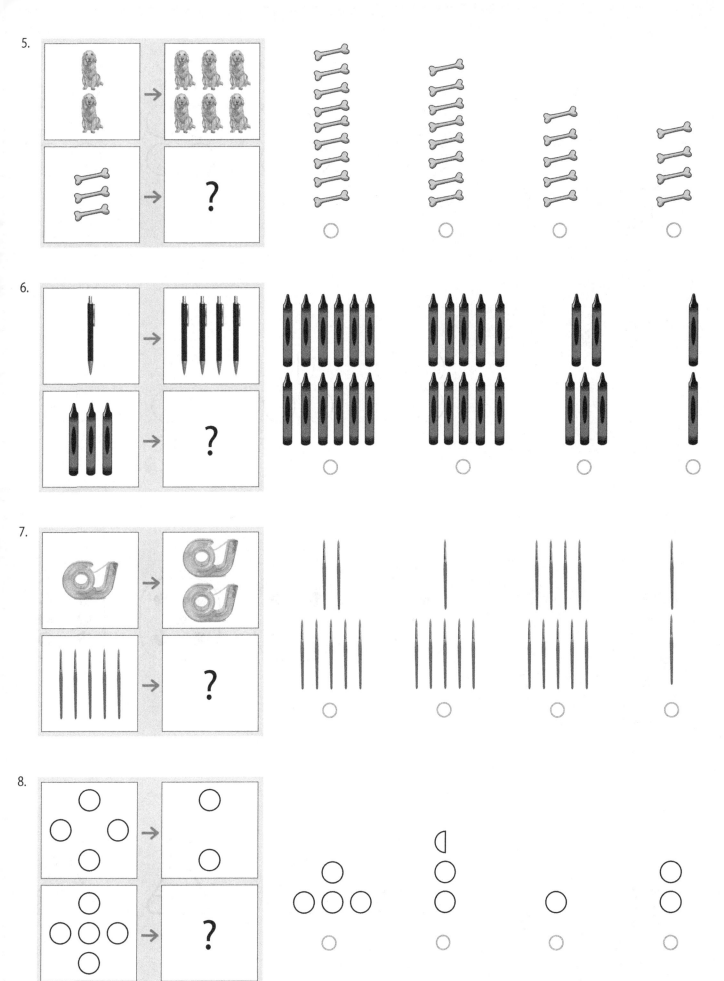

9.

10.

11.

12.

 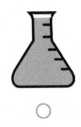   

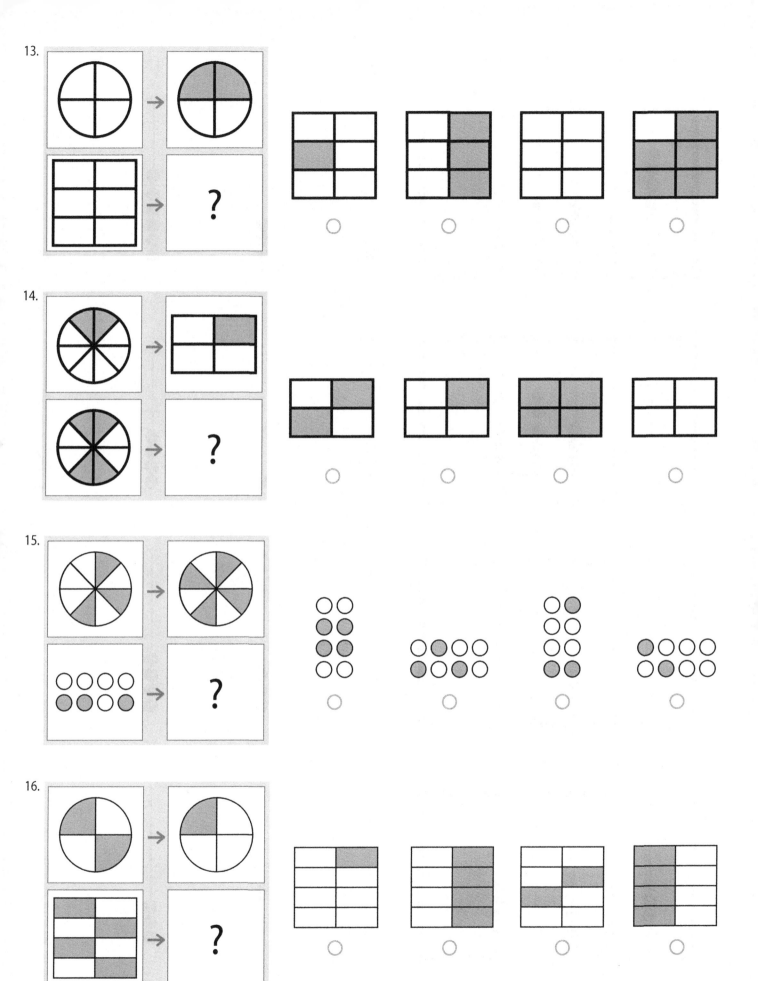

NUMBER SERIES

Directions: Which rod goes in the place of the missing rod to finish the pattern?

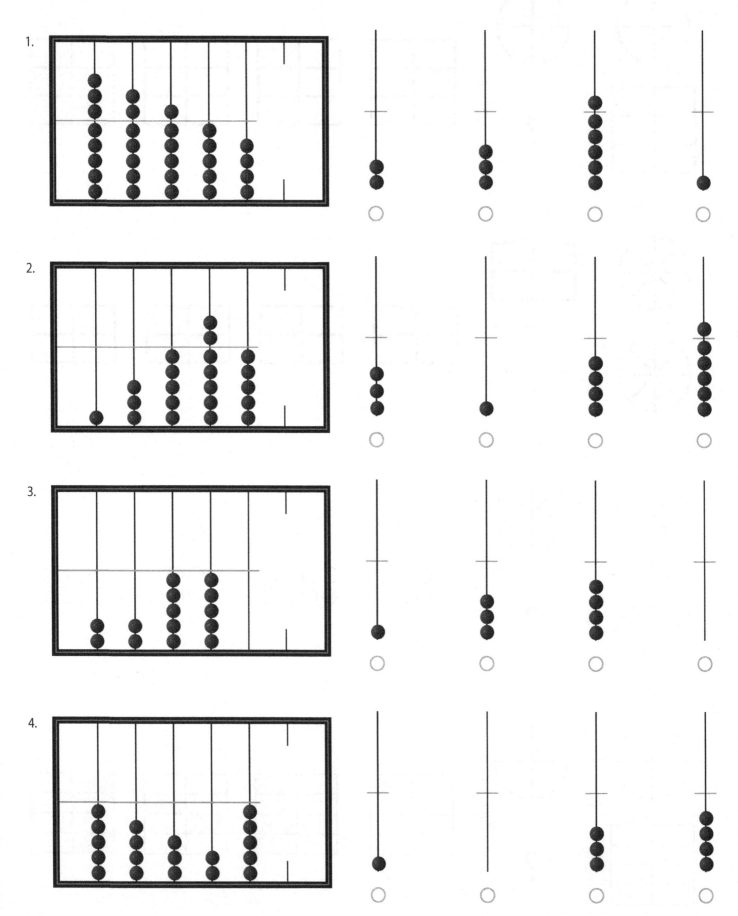

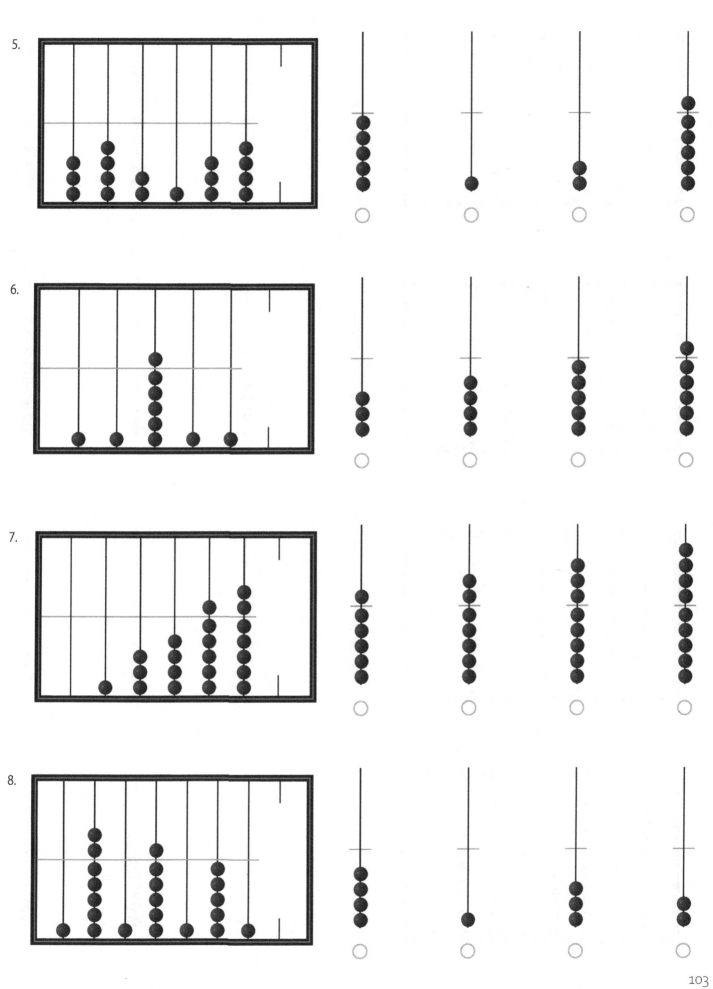

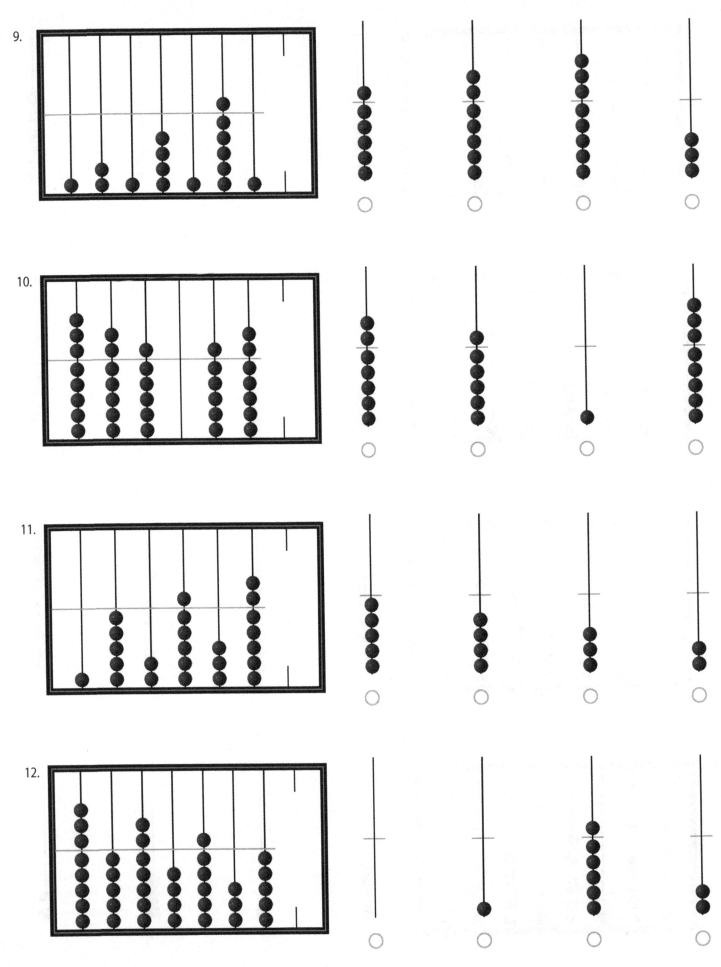

9.

10.

11.

12.

104

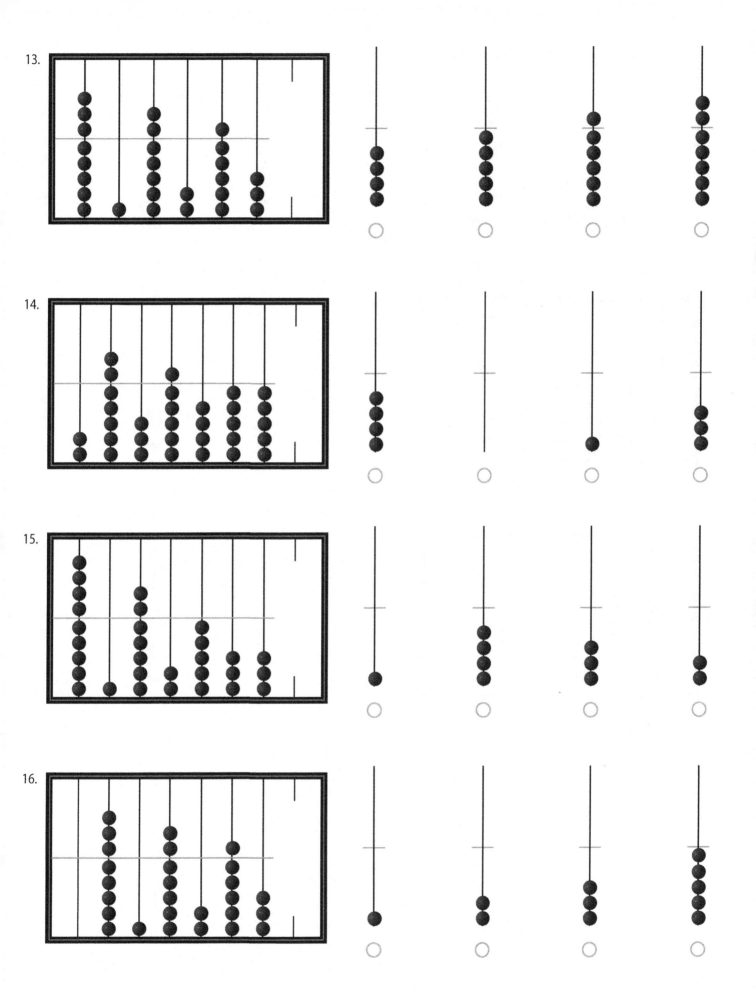

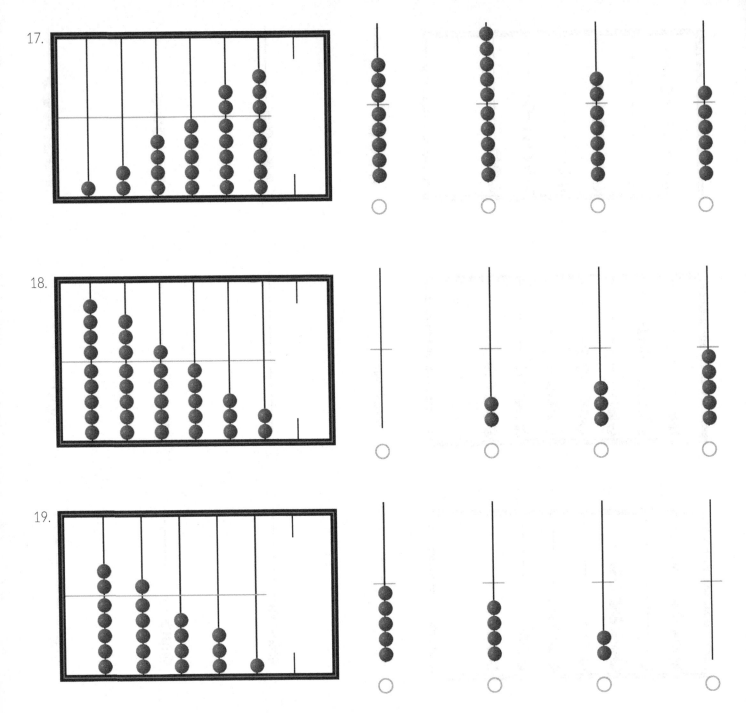

17.

18.

19.

- END OF PRACTICE TEST 2 -

GO TO www.SavantPrep.com FOR

• 10 FREE TEST PREP QUESTIONS

• A CHANCE TO WIN
2 FREE TEST PREP BOOKS

COGAT GRADE 1 COGAT GRADE 2 COGAT GRADE 3 COGAT GRADE 4 COGAT GRADE 5

ANSWER KEY FOR PRACTICE TEST 1

Picture Analogies (Practice Test 1) / Write the number your child answered correctly: _____ out of 18
1. C: food utensils on top; tools on the bottom
2. D: eyes are the main body part used with a microscope; ears are the main body part used with headphones
3. A: 3-D shape > object with this shape   4. D: utensil in first box is used to consume object in second box
5. B: object > same object put into a container   6. D: wheat is used to make bread; milk is used to make cheese
7. A: opposites (sad > happy; empty > full)   8. C: trees are used to make paper; corn is used to make popcorn
9: B: a book is made from sheets of paper put together; cabins are made from pieces of wood put together
10. A: animal > animal's man-made, contained home
11. B: cabins are made of logs; igloos are made of ice (note this is the reverse logic from #9)
12. D: number of wheels > number of dots on dice
13. D: flame is source of light in a candle; light bulb is source of light in lamppost
14. C: object > how you turn object "on"   15. D: things that travel in the air; things that travel on land
16. A: object added on top that covers the original item (a hat on the boy, a cushion on the stool)
17. C: shape in second box has the same number of legs as the animal in the first
18. D: slower, older version > faster, modern version

Figure Analogies (Practice Test 1) / Write the number your child answered correctly: _____ out of 18
1. D: middle shape gets bigger   2. B: colors reverse -OR- the shape groups in the left and right boxes switch
3. D: rotates 90 degrees clockwise   4. A: number of shape sides increases by 1
5. D: shape gets bigger and darker   6. C: shape is cut in half & right half shows
7. B: +1 shape (gray squares / white lines) from the first box   8. B: shapes switch position and colors
9. C: top 2 shapes switch position -OR- top shape moves to bottom
10. C: smaller middle shapes align horizontally -and- the outer & inner shapes switch design (zig zags on top, color on bottom)
11. B: black stars become white diamonds and vice versa & the shape underneath reverses colors (white to black in top set; black to white in bottom set)
12. D: in group of 3 shapes, outer & inner shapes switch position
13. A: smaller white shape appears alone; it changes from white to black and rotates 180 degrees
14. A: upper left & lower right shape switch   15. B: in the "domino" +1 circle on top, -1 circle on bottom
16. B: the shapes with the horizontal lines from first box remain & are white
17. C: number of arrow points > shape with same number of sides   18. D: rotates 90 degrees clockwise

Picture Classification (Practice Test 1) / Write the number your child answered correctly: _____ out of 19
1. C: worn on feet   2. D: insects   3. B: toys   4. A: hold liquid   5. D: flying insects
6. B: cold weather clothes   7. D: use electricity   8. A: have to do with birds   9. C: adult animals
10. D: pairs   11. B: provide light   12. C: wild animals   13. B: striped   14. A: transport many
15. C: lowercase vowels   16. D: used to cut   17. C: containers   18. B: grown on trees
19. A: lowercase consonants

Figure Classification (Practice Test 1) / Write the number your child answered correctly: _____ out of 18
1. D: cut in half   2. B: light gray   3. B: 5-sided shapes   4. D: pointing left
5. A: 3 arrow points   6. C: 3 shapes   7. B: 1 square is black   8. D: 1 square, 1 star, 1 circle
9. C: 2 of same shape next to each other & 1 different shape   10. A: 3 black shapes/2 white shapes
11. D: 1 of 3 sections black/2 sections gray   12. D: rectangle in middle   13. C: black line at same spot on arrow
14. D: 1 large shape & 2 smaller shapes of the same shape   15. B: larger shape & smaller shapes opposite colors
16. A: 2 black lines & 1 gray line inside   17. A: 7-sided shapes   18. D: half of shape (2 sections) are black/2 are white

Sentence Completion (Practice Test 1) / Write the number your child answered correctly: _____ out of 18
1. D   2. B   3. C   4. D   5. B   6. C   7. A   8. B   9. C   10. A   11. A   12. B   13. B   14. C   15. D
16. A   17. C   18. C

Paper Folding (Practice Test 1) / Write the number your child answered correctly: _____ out of 16
1. D   2. A   3. C   4. B   5. C   6. B   7. D   8. B   9. C   10. A   11. D   12. B   13. C   14. D
15. C   16. B

ANSWER KEY FOR PRACTICE TEST 1, CONTINUED

Number Puzzles (Practice Test 1) / Write the number your child answered correctly: _____ out of 22

1. B   2. D   3. A   4. C   5. D   6. A   7. C   8. D   9. A   10. B   11. C   12. B   13. A   14. C   15. C
16. D   17. A   18. B   19. A   20. C   21. C   22. D

Number Series (Practice Test 1) / Write the number your child answered correctly: _____ out of 17

1. B   2. B   3. D   4. A   5. D (every other rod = 0)   6. B (rods 1,3,5 = 1; rods 2,4,6, increase by 1 bead)

7. D (rods decrease by 1 until "2", then increase by 1)   8. D (every other rod, +2)

9. B (7-1-4-7-1-4-7)   10. C (rods 1,3,5,7 = 2; rods 2,4,6,8 decrease by 1 bead)

11. B (rods 1,3,5,7 decr. by 1; rods 2,4,6,8 incr. by 1)   12. A (rods 1,3,5,7 decr. by 1; rods 2,4,6,8 incr. by 1)

13. B (rods 1,3,5,7 incr. by 1; rods 2,4,6,8 incr. by 1)   14. D (rods 1,3,5 incr. by 1; rods 2,4,6 incr. by 1)

15. D   16. B (+1,+2,+1,+2, etc.)   17. C (+2,+1,+2,+1, etc.)

Number Analogies (Practice Test 1) / Write the number your child answered correctly: _____ out of 18

1. B (-5)   2. D (+6)   3. C (+7)   4. A (-5)   5. D (half)   6. C (double)   7. D (triple)
8. A (double)   9. C (triple)   10. B (quadruple)   11. D (half)   12. D (half)   13. B (half)   14. C (double)
15. D (half gray / half white)   16. A (+2 sections gray / -2 sections white)
17. B (7 objects (cookies/gifts, split 3 & 4, on 2 plates/2 tables)   18. D (5 objects, split 3 & 2, in 2 vases/ on2 plates)

ANSWER KEY FOR PRACTICE TEST 2

Picture Analogies (Practice Test 2) / Write the number your child answered correctly: _____ out of 18

1. B: vehicle > where vehicle travels   2. A: single thing > group of this thing joined together
3. D: similar function (used to water; used for light)   4. C: toy version > real version (boys; ducks)
5. A: both fruits; both vegetables   6. C: both are open; both are closed
7. B: food grown on vines; food grown on trees   8. A: shape with "X" number of sides > "X" number of beads
9. D: slower version > faster, motorized version   10. C: a baby needs milk to grow; a bush needs water to grow
11. A: single thing > group of similar things   (a baby gets milk from a bottle; a bush gets water from a hose)
12. B: water > large quantity of water in the ocean; corn plant > large quantity of corn plants on a farm
13. B: complete set > one single item from the set (bone, flower petal)
14. A: finished product > what it is made with (fence made with wood; shirt made with thread)
15. C: worker > object this worker uses to complete tasks at their job (a doctor uses a needle; a chef uses measuring spoons)
16. B: weather > child wearing clothing for that weather   17. D: worker > finished product (artist > painting; carpenter > wooden chair)
18. A: opposites (alive > dead; front > back)

Picture Classification (Practice Test 2) / Write the number your child answered correctly: _____ out of 18

1. D: utensils for eating   2. A: sweets   3. B: musical instruments   4. B: things used to carry
5. D: school supplies   6. B: cold things   7. B: used for measuring/ measurement "tools"
8. D: something to sit on   9. C: homes   10. A: real vehicles   11. B: animal homes
12. D: used to hit sports balls   13. C: uppercase consonants   14. B: animal feet   15. A: things worn on head
16. B: have wheels   17. B: hand tools (not electric/gas-powered)   18. D: measure time

Sentence Completion (Practice Test 2) / Write the number your child answered correctly: _____ out of 18

1. C   2. B   3. A   4. D   5. B   6. C   7. A   8. C   9. D   10. B   11. C   12. D   13. C   14. C   15. A
16. B   17. D   18. D

Figure Analogies (Practice Test 2) / Write the number your child answered correctly: _____ out of 18

1. D: top 2 shapes switch position -OR- top shape moves to bottom
2. A: center horizontal line added, top left & bottom right sections shaded
3. D: shapes reverse direction (right goes left/left goes right), then overlap, and turn white; triangles become squares and vice versa
4. D: shape rotates 180 degrees and becomes black and gray; the color of the original shape is on top (gray on top in top set; black on top in bottom set)
5. B: shape groups align vertically & get smaller; inner & outer shapes switch position & switch color

Figure Analogies, Continued (Practice Test 2)

6. A: black hearts become gray rectangles and vice versa & the shape underneath reverses colors (gray to black in top set; black to gray in bottom set)

7. C: shape group "flips"/becomes a mirror image; on the bottom, however, you don't notice the flip because of the black/gray circle arrangement

8. C: shape group faces opposite direction & 2 smaller shapes change from gray to white

9. D: Two shapes on left and right move to top and bottom; the colors of these two shapes switch with the middle shape

10. D: there are 2 shapes divided in half: a square and a smaller circle; the colors of the square halves switch & so do those of the circle halves

11. B: in the left boxes, there are 2 figures; the left of these 2 moves to right side of right figure and the 2 figures join

12. D: the colors change like this: gray > black; black > gray; white > wavy lines; wavy lines > white -OR- triangles 1 and 2 switch & triangles 3 and 4 switch

13. D: figure rotates 180 degrees & 1 more is added

14. C: circle switches color (gray to black/black to gray); diamond changes to heart, moves to upper right, and switches color (black to gray/gray to black)

15. B: 1st shape becomes 3rd; 2nd shape becomes 4th and rotates 180 degrees; 3rd shape becomes 2nd; 4th shape becomes 1st

16. C: top shape goes to middle & gets bigger; middle shape moves to bottom & gets bigger; bottom shape moves to top & gets smaller

17. A: figure "flips" vertically (to become a mirror image) & the smaller shape in the center moves above the larger shape group

18. D: circle group rotates 90 degrees clockwise & reverses color - see here: first: original figure; second: figure rotates 90 degrees clockwise; third: colors reverse black/gray

Figure Classification (Practice Test 2) / Write the number your child answered correctly: _____ out of 18

1. D: 3 "curve" down/ 1 "curves" up

2. C: straight-edged shapes (not rounded)

3. D: lines go from lower left to upper right

4. C: shape pattern: gray-white-gray (3 shapes)

5. C: the black curved shape is on the same point of the gray shape as the 2 shapes rotate together 90° counterclockwise

6. A: 2 different shapes

7. B: 4 shapes

8. C: as shape group rotates, the small octagon remains at the same point in relation to the arrow group

9. D: rounded shapes

10. D: as shape group rotates, the small triangle remains at the same point on the gray figure

11. C: divided in half

12. D: top shape has rotated 90 degrees clockwise

13. B: shape divided into 3 equal parts

14. B: 2 of the same shape vertically & horizontally inside the circle

15. C: the "minus" sign forms a tic-tac-toe (3 in a row) pattern inside the matrix

16. A: 2 white squares, 1 square with diagonal lines, 1 square with small shape inside

17. A: gray diamond has 1 star & 1 triangle inside & they are next to each other

18. B: in the 3 shapes (heart, square, rectangle), 1 is gray, 1 has dotted lines, 1 has diagonal lines

Paper Folding (Practice Test 2) / Write the number your child answered correctly: _____ out of 15

1. C   2. B   3. D   4. A   5. B   6. D   7. D   8. A   9. B   10. D   11. C   12. B   13. C   14. A   15. B

Number Puzzles (Practice Test 2) / Write the number your child answered correctly: _____ out of 18

1. C   2. A   3. D   4. A   5. B   6. B   7. D   8. A   9. C   10. B   11. A   12. D   13. A   14. C   15. B   16. D   17. A   18. C

Number Analogies (Practice Test 2) / Write the number your child answered correctly: _____ out of 16

1. D (-3)   2. A (+4)   3. C (half)   4. C (double)   5. A (triple)   6. A (quadruple)

7. B (+1)   8. B (half)   9. D (double)   10. A (double)   11. D (double)   12. A (almost full)

13. B (half become shaded)   14. A (one-fourth shaded in top set; half shaded in bottom set)

15. A (+1 gray section shaded / -1 white section)   16. C (number of gray sections decreases by half from left to right)

Number Series (Practice Test 2) / Write the number your child answered correctly: _____ out of 19

1. B   2. A   3. D   4. D   5. C (3-4-2-1-3-4-2)   6. D   7. D (+1,+2,+1,+2, etc.)

8. A (rods 1,3,5,7 = 1; rods 2,4,6, decrease by 1 bead)   9. C (rods 1,3,5,7 = 1; rods 2,4,6,8 increase by 2 beads)

10. D   11. B (rods 1,3,5,7 incr. by 1; rods 2,4,6 incr. by 1)   12. D (rods 1,3,5,7 decr. by 1; rods 2,4,6,8 decr. by 1)

13. B (rods 1,3,5,7 decr. by 1; rods 2,4,6 incr. by 1)   14. A (rods 1,3,5,7 incr. by 1; rods 2,4,6,8 decr. by 1)

15. B (rods 1,3,5,7 decr. by 2; rods 2,4,6,8 incr. by 1)   16. D (rods 1,3,5,7 incr. by 1; rods 2,4,6,8 decr. by 1)

17. B (+1,+2,+1,+2, etc.)   18. A (-1,-2,-1,-2, etc.)   19. D (-1,-2,-1,-2, etc.)

Made in the USA
Columbia, SC
23 November 2024